D1480379

Wherever You Go, There He Is

Wherever You Go, There He Is

100 TRUE MIRACLES OF FAITH

Plus True Stories
from Crossings Members

VOLUME ONE

CROSSINGS BOOK CLUB
GARDEN CITY, NEW YORK

Published by arrangement with Dorchester Media. Miracle of Faith stories first appeared in *True Story* magazine.

Published by Crossings Book Club, 401 Franklin Avenue, Garden City, New York 11530

Book design by Monica Elias

ISBN: 1-58288-163-4

Printed in the United States of America

In 1963, it was discovered that my second son was severely brain damaged. He was four years old at the time and up until this point he had been fine. I couldn't believe it! To this day we have no idea how it happened, but right then—even though my father was a minister, as were both my uncle and my brother—I turned my back on God.

My life had always been perfect. *How could He do this to me?* I wondered with despair. And finding no answer, I quit going to church and began drinking.

My dad had always told me, "When you find yourself in a fix and there's no time to pray, just whisper the name of Jesus." I forgot my father's advice until the summer of 1969. My eldest son—who was eleven at the time—had taken both swimming and diving lessons, and we were swimming together in a small lake my father owned. We'd swum across several times before, so on this day we decided to swim over and back as usual. But on our way back, my son gave out and panicked. He wrapped himself around me in a strangling grip and we couldn't move. I knew if he went down, I was going with him—we would both be drowned.

Then I remembered what Dad had told me so many times before. With a great effort I managed to pull my son off me while still keeping us both afloat, and then I said to him, "We must whisper the name of Jesus."

We were only in the middle of the lake and both of us were already worn out, and all we could manage to gasp was, "Jesus, Jesus," over and over again. But it worked. We both calmed down and made it safely back to the opposite shore.

That was the turning point for me—when I went back to the faith in which I'd been raised. It's been fifteen years since that near-tragic day, and when I look at my handsome son who will soon be twenty-six, I know I'll never forget my miracle or cease to praise the compassionate God that gave both of us the strength to make it across that lake.

—N.R., West Virginia

Around Christmas of 1976, my husband was hospitalized and was subsequently out of work for several weeks. Living on my salary was rough, and we were almost touching bottom.

My father is a Baptist minister, and every year at Christmastime we always got a list of needy children at the Miracle Hill Children's Home in Greenville. Many children are housed there, and it is a faith operation. Some children are orphaned and others are abused or neglected. The list gave the children's ages and sizes so we would know what to buy them for Christmas. We had always tried to help, but this particular year I didn't see any way we could afford to.

Several weeks passed, and it was one week before we were to go and carry the gifts to the home. I still felt strongly that we should sponsor a child, but I kept putting it off. Then on Wednesday night, during prayer meeting, my father announced that there were still some children left without sponsors. The gifts were to be taken to the home the following Sunday afternoon. I felt the Lord speak to me, and I pledged that night to sponsor two of the children, not knowing how my husband and I would pay for it.

That Friday, my husband and I went shopping and bought outfits and a toy for each of the children we had agreed to sponsor; the total bill was seventy dollars. I tried not to worry about the money, but I could not seem to help it. But the joy on the children's faces on Sunday made the sacrifice worth it.

The following Monday, my husband went back to his job. Then the following Friday, when he picked me up at work, he was wearing a huge smile. I asked what he was so happy about, and he pulled some money out of his shirt pocket. You know how much it was? Seventy dollars! His co-workers had taken up a collection to help him out, and that's how much they ended up with. Our sacrifice was rewarded, and those children were made happy. God does reward us for having faith and trusting in Him.

—T.E., South Carolina

One night my son was coming home from a party and he fell asleep at the wheel, flipping his truck over. My second son came and got me and we rushed to the hospital, only to hear the terrible news.

Upon examining him, the doctors told me that my son

shouldn't have survived. He'd broken his neck in five places and twisted his lower spine. The hospital wasn't equipped to handle his injury, so he was moved to a larger city hospital. The doctors there gave me the same diagnosis and didn't know if they could help him.

The doctors said they would try surgery, but nothing was guaranteed. They said my son could die, or he could come out of the operation paralyzed from the neck down.

By this time, I was so upset. I hadn't left the hospital once, for fear of my son dying while I was gone. I was pacing the floors, wringing my hands, and trying my hardest not to cry and fall apart. All of a sudden, a powerful feeling told me to see my pastor. I tried to push it aside because I didn't want to leave the hospital. But I knew it had to be done.

I went to see the pastor and we prayed together. He promised me he would say a prayer for my son in church on Sunday. I left there with a weight lifted from my soul, and somehow I knew my son would be okay.

My son went in for surgery and the doctor said he'd be in the hospital for a year of therapy. Amazingly, he was only in there for three months. He left the hospital on his own strength and without the help of any aide.

I'm very grateful for the knowledge and hard work of the doctors, but I know that it was the power of prayer that truly healed my son. I believe in God's miracles, and no one can tell me any different.

—P.W., Iowa

❖

M
y husband has always worked in noisy shops, and over the years he suffered a severe hearing loss. It had gotten so bad that he couldn't even hear me call from the second story of our house.

Two years ago my husband and I were working in the backyard. I was up on a ladder cutting away a vine that had become entangled in our cherry tree. My husband was running the lawn mower in the far corner of the yard.

Suddenly, the ladder gave a big lurch to the right, causing me to lose my grip. I caught on to a piece of the house, but every time I shifted my weight, the ladder moved a little more.

Slowly, fear started creeping into my mind as I thought of all the horrible things that could happen if I fell. I knew that calling out to my husband would be futile, because he'd never hear me over the noise of the mower. Tears formed in my eyes as I realized that my greatest fear had become a reality. As my throat closed up from fear I called out to the Lord for help.

All at once the mower stopped and I heard my husband calling to see if I needed help. I was so shocked he asked, because I was hidden from his view behind the cherry tree. There was no way he could've known I was in trouble.

Later, after my husband rescued me and we were discussing the incident, my husband told me that he thought he'd heard my voice calling him. It was then we knew that a miracle had taken place. We gave our thanks to the Lord for being the voice in my husband's ear.

Since we have always trusted in the Lord to help us in our

times of need, He couldn't have shown us more clearly that He is there to hear and answer our prayers.

—M.D., California

I was only six months pregnant—I couldn't be having my baby. *This can't be happening,* I thought to myself as another pain hit me. Suddenly, I felt my water break and realized that I was in labor.

The rest of the night was a blur. The trip to the hospital and the emergency surgery seemed like a nightmare. My baby was three months premature and weighed only two pounds. He had two holes in his heart and his lungs were filled with fluid.

A week after his birth the doctors came and told me that my baby had no chance of living. His veins had collapsed and they could no longer feed him. They wanted to remove the life support systems.

That night my husband and I went to the nursery to say good-bye to our son. Just one look at him and we knew he was dying. We got down on our knees and turned our son over to God.

We asked him to heal our baby if it was His will. If not, we asked that he go painlessly. But whatever God's will was, we were prepared to accept it. Miraculously, God heard our prayers!

The next morning the entire hospital was talking about the "miracle baby." My son was actually crying! He continued to improve and, many weeks later, we brought him home.

Today, as I look at my nineteen-year-old son who stands tall and strong, I thank God for this miracle. I truly believe that God answers prayers. All you need is faith!

—N.D., Tennessee

I was raised in a Christian home, but I always took God for granted. My family went to church every week, but God was never a part of my everyday life. I only prayed when I wanted something, but God never seemed to answer those prayers.

Even when I married and left home, I never thought about God. When my first child was born, I thanked God that she was healthy and then forgot about Him again.

We moved away from our city to a smaller town. My husband got a job at a resort, washing dishes, but we managed to make ends meet.

One day, my husband came home from work early. When I asked him why he was home, he said the resort was closing down for the winter and he'd been laid off. Times became hard for us. There were no jobs available, and we had to live on welfare and food stamps—they never stretched far enough.

We moved into subsidized housing and tried to prepare for winter. Our daughter was a year old and we were worried that we wouldn't be able to provide for her. My husband started spending his time in the bar.

One night, after I tucked my daughter into bed, I began to pray. I looked up from my prayers and saw my old Bible. I hadn't prayed in two years, but I decided to give it another try. I felt very peaceful that night and believed that God would answer my prayers.

Two days later, I saw some women looking around our apartment building. They knocked on a door down the hall, but no one was home. I told them they wouldn't be home until later. They told me they were from a church and they were here to give food out. They asked if I knew anyone who needed help. I told them that I needed help, and they gave me eight bags full of food, some clothing, and a Bible.

From that time on, they came every month and brought us basic necessities. I began going to church again, and felt peaceful, even in the face of an alcoholic husband. After four months, my husband began to realize what he was doing and went through rehabilitation. He even went to church with us.

It's been three years since then, and we're expecting our third child. I'll never forget the kindness of the church and how that one act changed my life. My husband has been sober for two years and he has a steady job that pays well. I realize now that God really does answer prayers, and I'll never again take Him for granted.

—K.S., Maryland

It was a beautiful spring day in May 1980. I was just sitting outside, enjoying the weather, when a car came flying into the driveway. It was my uncle, and I knew then that something was wrong.

8

He and my brother worked together at a sawmill in a nearby town, and my brother wasn't with him. I followed my uncle as he ran into the house where my mom and dad were.

He was very upset as he told my parents that my brother had been badly hurt. On the way to the hospital, he explained what had happened.

My brother and one of the other boys were tying down a load of timber with chains and a bucker. It seems that they had put a pipe on the bucker handle to get better leverage, and the pipe slipped off and the bucker handle came up and hit my brother in the face.

By the time we got to the hospital, the doctors had already begun surgery on him. When the surgeon came out to talk to the family, he said the bucker handle had crushed the right side of my brother's head, shattering his skull. The doctor had picked pieces of bone out of his brain. If he survived, the doctor said, he would not know anything or anyone, and he would be a vegetable; he would never be able to walk or talk again.

I couldn't imagine my brother that way. He was always strong, physically and mentally.

After two weeks, he was still unconscious. I was so afraid that he would never wake up. I'd go in and sit by him, talking and praying day after day.

One night I overheard my dad asking our preacher to have a special prayer for his son. When the preacher went into my brother's room, I closed my eyes and said a special prayer for my precious brother. I didn't care if he didn't remember me; I just wanted him to open his eyes, so I'd know if he was responsive. Sixteen hours after I said those prayers, my brother woke up.

It's been nearly twelve years since my brother was hurt. He is a walking, talking, loving miracle. He's blind in his right eye and can't hear with his right ear, and forgets small things at times, but there is absolutely nothing else wrong with him.

I know that God is the reason my brother is still here today, and I thank Him every day.

—J.M., Alabama

Five years ago I found myself at a very low and miserable point in my life. I had left an abusive marriage of six years and wasn't prepared for the single life. I reached for alcohol to ease the pain and shock.

I began drinking excessively. I drank in the morning to ease into the day before me. I drank at noon to keep the "giddy" feeling alive. I drank at night because it was dark and I was lonely. I abandoned responsibilities, friends, and living.

In a weak moment one day, I phoned my mother and told her what was happening in my life. I asked her if I could come home to try and collect myself, and she agreed.

Upon my arrival, my mother shared with me a strong feeling she'd had prior to my phoning: She was reading the story of the Prodigal Son in the Bible one morning, and something told her that I was the prodigal child. She didn't understand what it meant until I called her with my situation. She was happy that I'd come home for the celebration.

Unfortunately, it wasn't time to celebrate yet. I hadn't dealt with the things that had led me to drinking, and I began drinking again. Three months later I entered a treatment program. My life had become unmanageable and I saw no other alternative.

During my stay, my mother wrote encouraging letters. She reminded me of the Prodigal Son story and how she felt I was paralleling it. I didn't think too much about it until the day of my "hot seat."

A hot seat is something each person going through treatment must face alone after a designated time. It involves admitting all that one has done wrong and being healed. Afterward, a minister goes with the individual and prays for strength.

I finished my hot seat and followed the minister into a room. My head was pounding, and my eyes were swollen and red from crying. I cradled my head in my hands as the minister recited selected words from the Bible. Suddenly a few significant words caught my attention. I asked him if he was reading the story of the Prodigal Son. He said yes.

I couldn't believe it! I began crying, but they were happy tears now. I relayed my mother's feeling when she'd read that story six months earlier. For the first time in a long time, I knew everything was going to be all right. God had His hand in this and I was exactly where I was supposed to be.

—C.F., Montana

During one sad summer, I went through a shattering divorce. At twenty-three, with no skills or education and three small children, I felt my world falling apart.

My aunt wanted to help us out, so she invited the kids and me to move in with her. Then in October, my cousin and her family were having financial problems and needed to move in.

I had enough money saved to find my family a place to live, but very little left over. The children and I were soon down to any meal I could make inexpensively.

I realized I had to apply for welfare; at least then I could get food for my children. I was given a hard time at first because I was from out-of-state, but then they sent me to a church for a ten-dollar food voucher and said I'd have to wait a few weeks for my food stamps.

As the holidays approached, each night the children and I would take an evening walk to look at all the houses decorated for Christmas. One night during our walk, we went into a church. I sat and poured out my problems and tears to the Lord, and asked him to help me take care of my children. Then I spoke to the pastor. He listened with empathy as I cried, and said he'd mention my situation the next day during services.

A few days later I was returning home from another day of job hunting, and I suddenly stopped and stared at my front porch. It was covered with grocery bags filled with turkeys, vegetables, baked goods, fresh fruits, and even canned jam and fruit—from people whom I had never even met!

Then two nights before Christmas Eve, I noticed some more

bags and a Christmas tree on my porch. The bags contained wrapped gifts, toys, and candy.

Fifteen years have passed since then. I've received my high school equivalency diploma, and in six months I'll be graduating with a degree in criminal justice and sociology.

Though things have changed, I'll never forget where I once was, or the people who cared and gave with their hearts and prayers. That year I learned the true meaning of Christmas. It's not about making out our Christmas shopping lists or receiving the fancy new coat or the new dress and shoes.

Christmastime is the time to make lists of all the things we so very much take for granted and should be thankful for; but most important of all, it is the birth of Christ, who makes all things possible.

—S.O., Texas

It happened one Christmas Eve. My husband and I were going through difficult times then; he was out of work, and I had a job working evenings at a hospital nearby.

I tried to get the night off so that I could do the things that so many of us leave for the last minute, but since I had the least amount of seniority, I had to work.

One of the things I needed to do was buy a Christmas tree. We always left that for Christmas Eve, because most places that sold real trees lowered their prices that night.

My husband promised me that he would take care of things while I was at work, and that when I got off at 11:00 P.M., everything would be done—including buying and decorating a tree. I called home around 9:00 P.M. to see how everything was going, and became a little nervous when he hadn't gone yet to get the tree. He spoke with much confidence, though, and assured me that he'd have the tree before I came home.

When I arrived home a little after 11:00 P.M., the house was neat and tidy—but no Christmas tree was in sight! My husband was sprawled out on the couch and fast asleep. When I saw the dispirited expressions on the faces of my two older children, I could hardly contain myself. I marched down the hall and knocked on my friend's apartment door. I had to talk to somebody.

She tried her best to calm me down and get me to see that it wasn't the end of the world if we didn't have a Christmas tree. She said that I should appreciate whatever we did have, considering the circumstances. She finally convinced me to go to midnight mass with her, hoping it would make me feel better about everything.

In church, I prayed harder than I ever did before. I asked God to forgive me for my anger, and to help me be thankful for what I had.

As my friend and I were walking home from mass, a truck loaded with Christmas trees came speeding by. Suddenly, as we stared in amazement, one of the trees fell off of it and landed in the middle of the street. The truck didn't even stop. You can imagine our excitement as we ran and picked it up. It was one of the most beautiful Scotch-pine trees I'd ever seen—one that I couldn't have afforded even if we had gotten to the store on time.

I'll never forget that night. It serves as a reminder to never lose faith, for God is always there when you need Him and always on time.

—S.A., New York

I had never been a religious man; in fact, I never attended church, or even really pondered the existence of God. I was too busy trying to earn a better living, get ahead, and acquire nice things. I felt I was stronger than most, and that I had to rely on myself; no one, including God, would help me. I was wrong. A few years back, a drunk driver changed my outlook on life forever.

My wife and our fourteen-year-old daughter had been out grocery shopping. On the way home, less than three blocks from our home, a drunk driver ran a stop sign and smashed into the passenger side of my wife's car. The police estimated that he was traveling at sixty miles per hour. The drunk driver was declared dead at the scene from massive head injuries. My wife escaped with minor injuries, but our daughter had received the brunt of the impact.

The passenger door window had exploded in her face. Sixty-six stitches were required to close the cuts on her face, neck, and scalp. Her right arm and collarbone were broken. As the bucket seat collapsed toward the car's dashboard, my little girl's breastbone was cracked. Four ribs broke, causing a punctured lung. Her head struck the side of the steering column, fracturing her skull.

She was in surgery for more than six hours. My wife prayed

throughout the evening. I just kept telling myself that she was young and strong and a fighter.

When my daughter finally came out of surgery, the doctor informed us that her head injury was even more serious than they had first thought.

The following day, she lapsed into a coma, and her brain began to swell. Our doctor told us there was nothing left to do but pray. For the first time since I was a child, I prayed. I wept as I prayed to God to spare my daughter's life.

Three days later, she opened her eyes and told the nurse she was thirsty. The swelling had receded! Our doctor told us it was a miracle.

My daughter had a long road to recovery: several more operations and months of painful therapy. That was seven years ago. This year, she'll be twenty-one, and will graduate from college. I hold God in my heart every day now, and that's where He belongs! You see, He has not only given my daughter a second chance, but myself as well.

—L.F., New York

My son and his best friend were a mismatched pair. Everyone said so. They came from different worlds and had nothing in common. But somehow our studious, well-mannered son, a shy and sensitive boy who never once got into the scrapes other teenagers did, became fast and inseparable buddies with a notorious boy. Needless to say, my husband and I were as upset as we were bewildered.

We'd known this boy by reputation since he was a youngster. We'd heard of his childish pranks and, more recently, of his brushes with the law. Usually, these were minor offenses like trespassing and petty theft, but we heard whispers of worse things: fights and public drunkenness, disorderly conduct, unruly gatherings of his motorcycle gang.

My husband and I would wince every time a carload of rowdy boys screeched to a halt outside the house. We tried to explain to our son about bad company; warn him that even good, sensible people can be lured into wrongdoing if they associate with a bad crowd.

Our son would just put us off with smiles and vague reassurances. "He needs a friend like me," he'd say. He was never disrespectful or defiant, yet no matter what we said to him, he'd go to join that howling mob. It was usually after midnight that our son would finally come striding in, calm as always, flashing a grin to show us that all was well.

Then it came. That which all parents of independent teenagers dread the most, happened: the late-night phone call, the flat voice of the police officer, the news so hard to understand and accept through the fog of sleepiness and disbelief. "Your son's been in a serious accident . . . tried to run a railroad crossing, was smashed by a locomotive . . . car totaled . . . he and a companion are in critical condition, still alive . . ."

My husband and I were at the hospital in twenty minutes. There we learned that, as we had expected, his rowdy friend had been driving. The doctor told us that both boys were out of immediate danger; they had suffered similar injuries, however, and both were unable to move their legs. Only time would tell if the paralysis was permanent.

At our son's bedside, looking down at my son so small and vulnerable, I could no longer control my tears. He fixed his eyes on me, eyes that fought through fear and anesthesia and pain, and flashed a faint but plucky smile, a dimmed version of the soothing everything's-okay grin he'd given us the previous evening as he went out the door.

I put my hand on his arm. "I'm praying for you, honey."

He shook his head slightly. "No, Mom," he whispered with difficulty. "Pray for my friend. Pray for him."

I prayed all right. I prayed harder and more fervently and more humbly than I ever had in my life, but it was all for my own son. I couldn't pray for his friend. I couldn't push my way through the anger I felt at the irresponsible troublemaker whose recklessness had possibly ruined my son's life forever. I didn't have a single plea of mercy in my heart for this boy who had hurt my son, not a shred of pity, only a cold and unyielding bitterness.

So when it was this boy who recovered full use of his legs, to the astonishment of the doctors, while my son's paralysis remained and the prognosis worsened daily, I could feel no pleasure, no sense of victory. "How could God be so unfair?" I asked. "How could He reach down to heal the wicked and the guilty, while leaving the good and the innocent to suffer?" It became an obsession with me; the injustice of it made me nearly insane. The next time I saw my son, I exploded, weeping and pacing the room, pouring out my resentment and envy in a torrent of harsh and unkind words.

My son listened to my tirade quietly, and he reached out to grasp my hand. His face was pale and thin, but without a trace of strain or turmoil.

"It's as it should be, Mom," he said.

"But after all the praying I've done for you," I whimpered.

"I've been praying for my best friend." He smiled, his eyes lighting up with a strangely peaceful joy. "Don't you see, Mom? If God had one miracle to spare here, He spent it well by using it on the one of us who needed it most. My friend needed to be reminded of God's existence, power, and mercy. I didn't. I already knew. You and Dad have seen to that."

I suddenly felt as though I were burning with shame. Compared to our son's dignity and resignation in the recovery of his friend, my complaints seemed incredibly petty.

It took some time, but I was eventually able to share in my son's delight. Slowly, at first, reluctantly, we came to know his best friend, seeing in him what our son must have seen all along: the qualities of intelligence and sensitivity he had so carefully hidden under an exterior of sullen toughness. We helped him through his rehabilitation, and he now is a changed young man with a future.

Some would think our son wasn't so lucky, but thanks to his example, I know better now. Confined to a wheelchair, almost certainly for the rest of his life, he hasn't slowed down a bit. And in every important way he hasn't changed at all. Active in church and soon to enter college, he plans to earn a degree in psychology and devote his life to working with the handicapped. He'll be good at it, too, because he possesses a natural and intuitive wisdom rare and unteachable. After all, it was he who, all by himself, sensed that God is most likely to hear our prayers when we make them for the sake of others and not for ourselves.

—J.F., Ohio

When I was turning eleven, I wanted a pretty dress for my birthday more than anything else in the world, and I wanted to take a cake to school to share with my class like the other kids did—a cake with sparklers on it. Sparklers on cakes is an old Southern custom, and we were from Louisiana.

But my mother said, "Sweetheart, you know your daddy hasn't sent us a check in almost a year. We just can't afford a new dress—not even sparklers." Mama turned her back to hide her tears, but I could hear the tremor in her voice.

At Sunday school that week, Miss Raston, our teacher, showed us a picture of Jesus healing a blind man. "Jesus told us," she said, "that we must put our faith in God, and that we must believe. Jesus said, 'Ask, and ye shall receive.'"

Miss Raston went on with her lesson, but to myself, I thought: *God has deserted us. Mama and I believed in God and prayed to Him that Papa would find work and send for us, but it hasn't happened. God has forgotten us, and Papa has forgotten us, too.*

The Fourth of July came and went, a quiet one for us. Mama could not get a job, but pawned her watch when our money was almost gone. My birthday was only a week away and I felt miserable, but I tried to hide it from Mama.

God, I prayed on my knees, *please, oh, please, let me have a party dress for school. And, God, sparklers for my cake, too. Please, God. Please hear me.*

But I never believed my prayer would be answered. My faith was gone. First we were deserted by Papa, and now it seemed that God had deserted us, too. I began to sob, and ran down to the creek behind our house. I couldn't let Mama see my tears.

There by the creek, I began to cry again, but silently. Tears were streaming down my face as I began to make a castle in the sand—a big castle, where we could all be together and Papa would be king, and Mama the queen. I would be a royal princess and have nice things, and party dresses . . . and sparklers on my birthday cake.

My daydream ended as my fingers, deep in the sand, touched something—a stick, I thought. I dug deeper. Sticks, eleven of them, were there—the bottom ends of sparklers in their battered box!

My heart swelled to bursting and I jumped up and rushed home to tell Mama the wonderful news. She met me on the porch, her eyes shining, and spoke first.

"Baby, you won't believe it! We've heard from Papa! He's found work and has sent us a check! Oh, darling, you'll have your beautiful dress!"

God *had* heard my prayers, and He'd answered them. I knew then that He hadn't deserted us—and never would—as long as we believed!

—J.G., Georgia

In late October of 1982, my cousin and I decided we had to move to within commuting distance of a large city. We'd spent the previous six months looking for jobs which would bring in enough money for our families to live in relative comfort. She had two sons and two daughters. I had two daughters and a son. We agreed that we would try our hardest not to go on public assistance.

Still, the move was a scary proposition. We buoyed each other's courage by pointing out our great health, our youth, and our skill at commercial cleaning. We methodically wrote down our assets. We had between us one old station wagon which ran well, several changes of good clothes, and almost a thousand dollars, besides whatever we could get from selling our furniture. Surely, it would be enough.

We made careful plans. First we'd talk to our kids about our decision, then we'd explain to family and friends. In late November, I would drive the hundred and fifty miles to the city of our choice to rent a house, get the utilities turned on, and stock up on groceries. Then I'd return for the others.

All went well at first. We sold everything except the old black-and-white TV, but we decided I'd take it and everything else we could fit into the car on the first trip. That would give us more space during the actual move. My cousin bought a car-top carrier, and we happily contemplated the extra room it would give us.

My trip to the city was fruitful beyond my wildest hopes. By six o'clock that evening, I had rented an old, somewhat drafty, two-story house with six bedrooms, a stove, and a refrigerator. I then bought groceries and called my cousin from a pay phone to tell her and the kids the good news. I decided to sleep over at the new house and leave early the next day to bring them home.

We moved in on a Sunday. My cousin and I enrolled the kids in school on Monday and purchased the few supplies they needed. After the school bus picked them up the next day, we congratulated each other on our progress and decided we would fix up the place, scout out secondhand stores for furniture, then go out and find jobs.

That proved to be more difficult than we had anticipated. We applied for many jobs, but there were more people to compete with here. Our money quickly dwindled, and the second Wednesday in December, we realized we had no choice but to apply for public assistance. We had twelve dollars between us, so we had to apply for food stamps, too. The social workers saw no problem in our getting the help we needed, but they told us it could take up to thirty days before we got a dime.

Back home, we called all the places where we had put in job applications, then talked to our landlord, who assured us he'd let us pay the rent when we could. My cousin and I then discussed our seemingly insurmountable problem. Christmas was a few days away, and we had no money for gifts or a holiday dinner. We cried and agreed we'd have to tell the kids that night.

After dinner, we explained to them how bad our financial situation was, and we told them how it would get much better in a month or so. Then I dropped the bomb. Through tears, I told them there was no way we could celebrate Christmas the way other families did because we had no money.

To my surprise, my eight-year-old son came over and hugged me. He told me not to worry because Christmas was Jesus' birthday, and He wouldn't need any help to make Christmas come. He said Jesus hadn't had much money, either, so everything would be all right.

I prayed hard that night for God to help us reward the child's faith and somehow make Christmas special for all of them, even without money.

The next week, the telephone brought some eagerly awaited news. My cousin and I were both hired by the same janitorial company. She'd be working days, and I'd be working the graveyard shift. We'd need only one car, and one of us would always be with the kids. We gave thanks for what we felt was our salvation. There would be no paycheck before Christmas, but we were productive wage-earners again. The kids were overjoyed.

Late in the evening on December 22nd, the doorbell rang. As I walked to the front door, I heard a car start up and drive away. I opened the door. There was no one on the porch, but when I looked down, I cried out in surprise and joy. There by the door were three boxes of food, including a turkey and all the trimmings. Written in black marker on all the boxes were the words MERRY CHRISTMAS The message was an understatement.

The next evening, the doorbell chimed again. My cousin and I both went to the door. Standing on the front porch were two young women dressed in red-and-green elf suits, complete with pointy shoes. One of them put an envelope into my hand and said, "Merry Christmas." They hurriedly left as I mumbled my thanks.

I stepped back inside and opened the envelope. It contained five crisp new twenty-dollar bills. My son, who was standing in the doorway, grinned and said, "Didn't I tell you, Mom?"

Through the years since that Christmas, not one of us has ever lost faith in God. That year proved to us that there is nothing He can't do.

—K.K., Montana

Wiping my hands on my paint-smeared jeans and pushing a straggling piece of hair from my face, I answered the doorbell. My eyes beheld five neighborhood children under one large umbrella. Mischievous grins lit their faces, and I could tell that they were hiding something behind their backs. "Happy May Day," they said in chorus and handed me a "basket" full of construction-paper flowers they had made. Of course—it was May Day. I had forgotten. But the children hadn't.

Going back to my work with a lighter heart, I thought about my special relationship with children and how it had come about. I had two young sons and was expecting another baby when the church that I attended decided to take part in a program called "Fish." I thought at first that I wouldn't volunteer, but I couldn't refuse.

I decided that even with a new baby I could visit shut-ins. They probably would enjoy seeing a baby. I signed the sheet to visit shut-ins and promptly forgot about it as things got even busier in my life. I had two false alarms before the real thing. Yes, it was a daughter! But not a healthy, normal daughter. It was off to the children's hospital for surgery. She died two weeks later.

My heart grieved for my baby. I didn't eat, and I didn't sleep. I didn't want to be with my friends anymore. And, especially, I didn't want to go to church anymore.

Finally, in my darkest days, I packed away the baby clothes, thinking it might help if I didn't have to look at them. I was carrying the box down to the cellar when I dropped it. Something came over me, and suddenly I was sobbing and stomping all over those clothes. When I finally became aware of what I was doing, I sat down on the floor, still crying, and asked God to help me.

No flashes came from heaven to let me know that He had heard, but as I went back upstairs, the phone rang. The call was a reminder of my promise to visit shut-ins. I didn't want to, but something told me I'd better. After all, I *had* volunteered. And maybe, just maybe, it would take my mind off that terribly empty, aching spot in my heart.

The two ladies I was assigned to *had* both lost children. But while one still grieved fifty years later, and had become a bitter, self-centered recluse, the other had devoted her life to making children happy.

It was as if God were saying, "There they are. Which one do you want to be like?" Which one, indeed! I realized which way I had been heading and quickly reversed my course. And so now I stand, with my May Day flowers in my hand, realizing how lucky I was that I'd asked God for help on that dark day so long ago.

—M.A.M., New York

Last year my neighbor lost her husband from a sudden heart attack. They had just celebrated their twenty-fifth anniversary and had been planning a long-awaited cruise. The neighborhood was stunned. I think at first no one wanted to believe what had happened. But we learned to accept it—everyone but my neighbor, that is. She was emotionally destroyed by his death.

She and I had always been very close. We had often shopped or had lunch together, and our children, now either married or away at school, had been playmates. After her husband's death, however, she stayed secluded in her room and refused to see family and friends. She had always depended heavily on her husband for all major decisions and had never even learned to drive a car or handle their finances. And now, when she needed us most, she just turned us away.

At first, I respected her wishes and left her alone. But then the situation began to eat away at me. Why was I abandoning such a good friend in her hour of need? It certainly wasn't the Christian thing to do! So I turned to God in prayer; I knew He would show me the way.

Two months passed without any change. One evening after supper I went for a drive to think about the problem. As I drove through a small town, I noticed a little white chapel. On an impulse, I stopped and went in. The late evening sun streamed through the stained-glass windows, and candles glowed softly around the altar. I knelt there and prayed earnestly for my neighbor's recovery and for a way to help her find a new way of life.

When I left I felt stronger, confident that God would help *her realize* that *her* life wasn't over, that her husband wouldn't have wanted her to suffer so. After I got home, I told my husband about the church and my prayers. He agreed that it had been the right thing to do. He added that my neighbor was certain to snap out of her depression now that I'd asked God for help.

My phone rang the next morning, and my neighbor asked if I had time for a cup of coffee! I was shocked at her grief-ravaged face and loss of weight. She confided that she had awakened during the night suddenly feeling much stronger and no longer so completely alone. She said that she had just made an appointment for lessons at a driving school, and she asked if I could help her practice. I was so happy! God had answered my prayers! I knew now that she would make it.

Three months later, her new driver's license sat propped against the sugar bowl as we had our coffee. Since then, she's been taking bookkeeping and money-management courses and has put her gardening skills to use by working in a florist's shop.

Best of all, she has formed a support group for other widows. She's made new friends and discovered that she has unexpected strengths and talents.

I am convinced that her sudden recovery was more than mere coincidence—it was indeed a miracle of faith. Remember, God hears all our prayers—and answers them!

—E.L., New York

I stood in front of the glass in the Isolation ward of the pediatric unit, my heart filled with dread. Behind the wall of glass that separated me from my baby, the doctor was busy giving her an extensive examination. It seemed like an eternity before he finished and came through the door toward my husband and me. What he told us made my legs turn to jelly, and I began to shake uncontrollably. My beloved baby girl had salmonella poisoning and her fever was 105 degrees. If it didn't break soon, permanent brain damage would occur.

My husband stood beside me as the doctor delivered the news, his arm around my waist. If he had not been there, I am sure I would have sunk to the floor.

After the doctor had left, my husband and I stood and watched our eight-month-old daughter through the glass. Her beautiful hair had been shaven off, so the intravenous needle could be inserted into her temple. Another needle had been inserted into her tiny ankle. Ice bags and sand packs surrounded her to keep her from moving.

I began to weep hysterically, knowing in my heart that our only child was dying . . . and we weren't even allowed to be near her. A nurse approached and informed us that we should go home. There was nothing we could do. She told us that only time would tell if our daughter would survive. "All I can tell you to do is pray," she said.

We were not churchgoers, though my grandparents were very religious. The idea of really praying had never occurred to us. The nurse's words seemed to be just a figure of speech.

Later that night, the doorbell rang and when I opened it, there stood my grandparents' minister. I invited him in, and he told us that my grandmother had asked him to come by and pray with us. My husband and I looked at each other, remembering the nurse's words. We allowed the minister to pray with us, and then he left, saying he would check with us the next day. "I'll be praying for her," he said as he left.

For the next two days, there was still no change in our baby's condition. Our doctor met us the second evening around seven o'clock, at the hospital. "If there's no change by midnight, I'm afraid there is no hope. Even now, I feel she cannot survive without permanent brain damage. All I can tell you to do is pray."

Once again, my husband and I looked at each other. We'd been hearing a lot about prayer lately. I went directly to the phone in the hospital hallway and called my grandmother. "Can you and Grandpa come to the hospital right away?" I asked. "Call your pastor and ask him if he can come too, please," I continued.

In twenty minutes, my grandparents and the minister were at the hospital. The nurses directed us to a small waiting room so we could have some privacy. Soon, other members of my grandparents' church began to come in, until the small room was crowded with people. We all joined hands, and the minister's deep voice led us in prayer.

We were still praying when the doctor entered the room. His face was creased with worry, and my heart once again filled with dread. "The baby's fever has broken," he told us. "She seems to be out of danger, but we don't know yet if any permanent damage has been done."

After he left, we once again began to pray. We thanked God for His mercy and for healing our baby. We asked Him to make it a total healing so she wouldn't suffer any permanent damage.

Our baby daughter is twenty years old now, with no signs of the illness of so many years ago. She is as beautiful now as she was then, and when I look at her, I still thank God for healing her. What beautiful memories I would have missed, had she died that night that we prayed. I thank God for answering our prayers, and I thank Him for giving me the wisdom not to underestimate the power of prayer.

—M.A., Ontario, Canada

After three years of trying, my husband and I had finally conceived. Throughout the first seven trouble-free months of pregnancy, I felt great. Every day was filled with dreams and plans for our future with the unborn miracle I was carrying.

As time wore on, however, my body began to swell and in my eighth month, I had to be admitted into the hospital. I was informed that my labor must be induced immediately or I might risk losing my baby. With my husband by my side, twenty-two hours later, I gave birth to a six-pound baby boy. His head was terribly distorted, and he was a deathly blue. Within moments, my son was rushed into intensive care. By evening, his temperature had soared, and his life was hanging perilously.

My son had an infection which is fatal in fifty percent of the cases. He was paralyzed on one side, and as with most cases, within twenty-four hours he had developed spinal meningitis. His head was still distorted by the forceps, and it was discovered that his brain had actually been bruised by his violent entrance into the world.

There was a tube inserted into my baby's nose and a tiny needle embedded into the skin of his forehead. He had patches connected to his chest to monitor his heartbeat, and to my horror, in the places where the patches had been moved, his thin skin had been torn away with the tape, leaving painful, open sores.

For eight months, he had stayed curled up, safe, warm, and free from pain and suffering. Now he lay in constant pain from the needles and from the sores. And the doctor had said that he was surely experiencing severe headaches due to the brain bruise.

In my room, I begged God to end my baby's suffering. I must have stayed on my knees for over an hour. But when I rose, I rose with new strength and a serenity that I had never known before.

I rushed into my son's hospital room and I assured him that everything would work out. I knew that he didn't understand the words, but I liked to believe that he understood the peace that I felt.

My son was healed. But then, our faith took us even further.

My son's doctor said that my boy would never be right. He said that we should prepare ourselves for years of special classes and special teachers and not to expect too much of him.

Obviously, he didn't know the Great Physician. My son is now in the third grade. He has continuously remained on the Honor Roll. He reads everything he can get his hands on. Math comes quite easily to him and he spells better than I do!

We have learned that there is nothing you can't accomplish with a little bit of faith and a whole lot of love.

—T.N., Florida

When I was a child, Grandma's favorite expression was, "You must have faith." It was Grandma who taught me my prayers and took me to church. Her strong faith in God was a part of her, woven into the fabric of her entire life.

On their first anniversary, Grandpa planted a maple tree in the backyard, a gift to Grandma. The tree was very special to them.

The years went by. All five of their children and all of their grandchildren spent many birthdays, holidays, and other family occasions under "Grandpa's tree." There were picnic tables, chairs, and swings there always ready to use.

When Grandpa was fifty-six, he suddenly took sick. As he got weaker each day, a strange thing happened. His tree began to lose all its leaves even though it was early June, the time trees usually bud. Soon most of the branches became brittle and began to break off. Grandma called in a tree expert who said nothing could be done—the tree was dying.

So was Grandpa. Within a few short months he was an invalid, unable to sit up. He lay on a bed by the window and watched as his tree withered, day by day.

"It will get better soon." Grandma smiled.

"No," Grandpa said softly, "it won't."

"You must have faith," Grandma insisted. "You're going to get well soon, too." Grandpa looked at her with so much love on his face that I had to turn away, tears flooding my eyes. He, best of all, knew how strong Grandma's faith was, how strong her belief in prayer.

He said in a weak voice, "I love you."

Grandma held his hand, her eyes echoing his words back to him.

On a cold December night, Grandpa died. I sobbed, inconsolable, while Grandma held me close. Calm, her face serene, she comforted me. "Have faith. It's God's will."

I felt hot anger. Why was it God's will to take a good man like Grandpa, leaving Grandma and me alone? Bitterness and grief stayed inside me—a heavy lump.

Sunday morning came and Grandma dressed to go to church. "Ready?" she called out to me.

"I'm not going."

Grandma was shocked. Never in her life had she missed hearing mass on Sunday.

"It will do you good to pray," she said softly.

"God didn't answer my prayers to make Grandpa well. He's dead, just like his tree."

"Perhaps God answered your prayer, but it wasn't the answer you wanted," Grandma scolded, gently. "You must have faith that He knows best."

In spite of all her pleading, I refused to go to church. Finally Grandma went alone, her face sad.

December dragged by slowly, then January and February. Each day, when Grandma and I looked out the window, we saw Grandpa's tree, black and bare, with an odd green mold growing up the trunk.

"Call someone to come and cut it down," I said harshly. Grandma shook her head stubbornly.

Finally March came, bringing the first breath of spring. I stared out the window morosely one morning, missing Grandpa. A big lump still seemed to be in my throat, all the time. Suddenly my eyes widened. I couldn't believe what I saw.

"Grandma, come look!" I cried out, excited. "Look at Grandpa's tree."

Grandma hurried to the window. The tree that had been dead and bare yesterday was now covered with soft green buds. The black color and mold were completely gone—it looked healthy and vigorous again.

Suddenly Grandma started to cry as if her heart was breaking. Since Grandpa's death she hadn't shed one tear, now it seemed she couldn't stop crying. Finally, wiping her eyes, she smiled at me.

"Can't you see? This is God's way of telling us that Grandpa is starting a new life with Him, just as the tree is starting a new life here. Someday we'll all be together again." Unwavering faith made her plain face glow with a shimmering beauty.

Grandpa's tree is now shading his great-grandchildren as they swing and play under its branches, with Grandma watching. I learned a lesson that March day that will stay with me all my life. Grandma was right. You must have faith!

—M.M., New Jersey

As a young girl I lived in the country. It was so beautiful, so safe. It was there that I was at peace with myself. Then one day my whole life changed; my father had gotten a job in the city. We had to move in less than a week. I was terrified!

I had said good-bye to all my dear friends and neighbors. As my folks were loading the last of our boxes onto our truck our pastor arrived. He talked with my folks a few minutes before walking down to the creek where I was sitting. We talked about all the beauty in God's wonderful world. It was going to be the hardest of all to say good-bye to my pastor. He had guided me through so many things in my life, the good times as well as the bad.

"I have a gift for you," he said as he handed me a small package. When I unwrapped it, I found a very dainty hand-carved cross. In its middle was a beautiful dove carved of stone with a rose in its beak. "It's very beautiful, Pastor," I said. "But why the rose?"

His eyes twinkled for a moment before he answered me. "I carved the cross out of dogwood like Christ's cross. The dove symbolizes eternal peace, which I hope you will always have. And the rose, my dear, sweet child, is you—delicate, gentle, one of God's creations. Please always remember your love for the Lord.

The cross is my gift to you. I hope you will always remember an old pastor who shares your love of the country."

After thanking him and saying good-bye, we loaded up and left for the city. I was sitting on the bed of our truck, holding my little package of love from a kind, old man. I was silently crying as I watched the countryside slipping by us. We were almost to the city, crossing an old bridge that led to the highway, when a car coming too fast almost crashed into us head-on. My father veered hard to the right to avoid hitting it. When he struck the guardrail, my little cross fell into the river. Luckily, no one was hurt and we made it to our new home in the city.

Ten years later, I had learned many things about city life. I had graduated college and was working as a bookkeeper in a sporting-goods store. I had learned how to survive in the city, although even after all that time, I still missed the country. I also learned that a lot of city men weren't what they said they were and could say "I love you" as easily as stating the time. I wanted to settle down, but I was still afraid. I had trusted too easily in the past.

One day I was daydreaming during my lunch break when a man walked in. He was tall and muscular and dressed in casual clothing. "I'm sorry, we're closed for lunch," I said. "A salesperson will be back in fifteen minutes, if you'd like to wait." He told me he'd wait because he needed some camping gear.

He introduced himself and as he waited, we started talking about the country. Before I knew it, I had accepted a date with him.

We got along great until one day, six months later, he said, "I love you. I want to spend my life beside you. Will you marry me?" I didn't know if I could trust him, but by then I had fallen deeply in love with him.

"Please, just give me some time to think," I said. Although a little taken aback, he agreed.

He gave me one week. At the end of the week we would go camping and I would give him my answer. During that time I prayed like I had never prayed in my life, for guidance, for some kind of sign. I knew God would lead me to do what was right.

We were walking along the sand by the river where we had set up camp. I was all finished setting up the camp. By now I knew it was getting late and I had to give him my answer. But I didn't know yet; God hadn't given me a sign.

I sat in the sand while he jogged down the riverbank. When he came back he sat down beside me and opened his hand. "Look what I found down the way. It's a little beaten up, but I think it's kind of pretty," he said.

My eyes filled with tears as I looked down at my little cross of so long ago. It was broken in places, but the dove with the little rose was still intact. God had answered me in a way I could not doubt.

My husband and I have been married for two years now. As I write this our daughter is sleeping in her crib and I hear the roosters crowing in the barnyard. I hope that God will guide your life as well as he did mine.

—P.H., Indiana

The bitter bite of winter hit me in the face on that gloomy day as I answered the knock at the door. Who'd be out on a day like this? It was even cold inside with the heat turned down to save money. But the worst coldness was the awful depression that had gripped me and wouldn't let go. If I didn't pull out of it, I wouldn't even be able to look for a job. Alone with a family to support, I couldn't bear the thought of a foster home for my children. It was out of the question.

Our carefully hoarded money was nearly gone, but we had a good supply of food from Christmas donations. However, I was so humiliated, I couldn't accept any more charity. Angry and terrified and weary of constantly expressing appreciation, I knew if God didn't do something, nothing was going to get done.

Help me, I'd begged. It wasn't much of a prayer, but it took all the faith I had. I sure hoped it would get above the ceiling. I was desperate. The lady at the door was nicely dressed, but she was so cold her eyes watered. "Hello. I live down the street. Our kids go to school together. I'm selling a line of home-care products. May I leave a catalogue and come back for your order?"

I felt hysteria rising. *My order?* I couldn't even afford a sponge! Just buying milk was hard enough, and the best I could do for cleaning products was a can of cheap cleanser. But it was freezing out and I couldn't just turn her away. "I can't afford to buy anything now," I said. "But won't you come in and warm up and have something hot to drink? We're new here and I haven't had any visitors."

She seemed grateful for the coffee, but I noticed her expression as she eyed the breakfast leftovers. She must be hungry. But it was still early. Maybe she hadn't had time to eat.

"I never eat until I've fed the baby and the children have left for school," I said. "There's plenty left. Why don't you join me?" A look of astonishment crossed her face. Then I noticed her tears were real and not from the cold. Her eyes overflowed and for a moment she couldn't speak. As I set a plate in front of her my smile changed to a look of curiosity.

"Thank you so much," she stammered, wiping her eyes. "I thought I could sell this stuff, but I'm not doing very well. My husband has left us and we have no food or money. Last night we went to bed hungry. But when I left the house this morning I said, 'Lord, you know my needs.' And I know He does."

You too? I thought. I felt a sudden surge of reckless energy, a combination of rage and determination. Standing, I flung open the freezer door. "I'm broke, too," I said. "Not even a dollar for the offering plate, and that's bad. But if there's one thing we have it's food. Christmas donations. Isn't charity just terrific?" I started filling a bag with frozen meat and vegetables. "Easy come, easy go!" I shrugged, but my laughter was born of an inner rage that we both could be in such a fix and the world could just keep on turning.

"Oh, no, I can't take your food!" she protested.

"Don't be silly," I said. "I'm going to find a job and we'll be okay." I felt a surge of energy bubbling up inside as my depression began to lift.

"Please help me," I begged. "Can't you see I'm tired of taking and need to give just to feel human again? Here, take this, and I'll give you something for today that's already cooked. The kids will bring it all down to you after school. I need you worse than you need me. Count on it."

Suddenly we were both laughing. "Isn't it ridiculous?" I said. "Giving and receiving are so natural and easy when you both have enough, and so hard when you don't. And it's so much easier to give than to receive."

"More blessed, too," she said, smiling. "Now I see why."

That day a friendship was born and God met the needs of two people in response to a faint, wordless cry. I was again reminded that He works in mysterious ways, not always giving exactly what we ask for but always, in His wisdom, providing what He knows we really need.

—J.H., Texas

I had been waiting to hear from my older daughter, who had recently separated from her husband and was living in a small city several hundred miles away.

It seemed strange that she hadn't written or called for so long. She had no phone, and I had not seen her in a year. I immediately made plans to travel by bus to visit her. My younger daughter, realizing how worried I was, offered to accompany me.

After many hot and exhausting hours on the bus, we finally arrived at our destination, and checked into a hotel. From there we took a cab to my daughter's address, but there seemed to be no one home in her apartment. We questioned her neighbors, who said that she no longer lived there. They told us the owners of the apartment might have her new address, and gave us the address of a furniture store they owned.

Wearily, we called another cab, as there was no type of public transportation in town. When we approached the owners, they gave us an address my daughter had left behind. My heart sank as they told us she had been having mental problems.

The next morning we walked to the new address, only there

was no such place! We spent many hours knocking on doors, armed with a photo of my daughter, only no one recognized her.

Bewildered, we hurried to the post office to see if she had made a change of address, but she had left none. Next we decided to try her last place of employment, but my daughter no longer worked there.

A policeman told us he had seen my daughter a few weeks earlier in the vicinity of the furniture store and the gas station.

The next day, we went to the gas station and inquired if anyone had seen my daughter. They had! I intended to stay on that avenue, if I had to walk back and forth until nightfall. Unfortunately, I became overheated with the sun beating mercilessly down upon me. So I asked the furniture-store owner if I could rest inside. He said yes.

It seemed I had only been there, waiting and hoping to see her, about thirty minutes. Then I caught a glimpse of a familiar figure. I ran out of the store and started yelling my daughter's name. She started running toward me.

Unfortunately, after a few minutes of talking with her, I sadly realized that my daughter was going through a nervous breakdown. It seemed that an unknown intruder had entered her former apartment at night, beating and raping her at knifepoint. He had threatened to kill her if she reported the incident to the police. She had left her apartment without telling anyone of her true whereabouts. She said she'd been planning to write to me.

She is now living a short distance away from me. My daughter is slowly picking up the pieces of her life, and taking one day at a time.

It was a true miracle of faith that led my daughter back to us, since the chances of finding her were so remote.

—M.S., Wisconsin

When my husband was in his last year of college, money was tight. And we certainly hadn't done things the easy way. We already had two little girls, but although it was a struggle, we were determined to get my husband through school.

That is why I was totally distressed when I learned I was pregnant—again.

Nobody loves babies more than I do, but until you've had an unplanned pregnancy, you can't imagine how devastating it can be. After all, I *had* a baby. She wasn't even two yet. She had been constantly sick for the entire year. My other child was only four. We were broke, we were struggling, and I was exhausted.

I knew that my husband was as worried as I was, but he tried to be positive and supportive. One thing that really bothered me was telling my dad. He was constantly concerned about our finances and about my health. I was sure he'd hit the ceiling.

When I finally worked up the nerve to break the news, Dad shook his head and smiled. Then he asked me how I would feel if the baby was another little girl.

I had a green-eyed girl and a blue-eyed girl. I didn't say it out loud, but I thought it would be awfully nice if I had a brown-eyed boy. Hidden in the bottom drawer of my dresser, I kept a little blue sailor suit—just in case.

I guess I thought I'd seen my miracle when my baby boy was born and his eyes were brown. But it was just the beginning. We had a name picked out for him, but at the last minute we changed our minds and named him after my dad.

My dad was delighted with the baby but, of course, he was delighted with all three of the children.

Then two unexpected things happened. First, I had to have an emergency hysterectomy, and I realized that if I hadn't had my little boy when I did, I'd never have had him at all. And then, when my son was just a few months old, my dad passed away suddenly.

At first I was too deep in mourning to see things in perspective, but as time healed my wounds, I began to be grateful for the time I'd had with my father and all that he'd meant to my children. I was thinking just that one day as I sat on a blanket with my baby son, kissing his toes and telling him stories. "I'm so glad your grandpa got to meet you," I told him. "I'm so glad you came before he died."

And then, I remembered something clearly. When I was in high school my dad had had a mild stroke. The thought of losing him had thrown me into a panic and I had gone to a little chapel in our neighborhood to pray for him. On my knees in the little church I had begged God to let Dad live long enough to see me married, long enough to see all of my children. Nine years later, God had honored that prayer, sending me my last child before He called my father home. God had perfect timing, in spite of me.

—J.J., Texas

erry was in the army in Canada when we got married. But soon after he got his release, we moved to the United States. He got a job installing power lines for an electrical company. It meant climbing high poles and working with high-voltage wires, and it was dangerous. But Gerry said the money was excellent. Then one day Gerry's pal had a bad fall and injured his back. Then we decided to return to Canada. Worrying that the same thing might happen to Gerry was no way to live. And, by then, we had a baby daughter, Andrea, to think about.

We went to live near his folks in a little town at the mouth of a wide river in Canada. There was good fishing and marshes and woods for hunting. Gerry started working with a construction company and was away all week. When he did get home, he'd go hunting or fishing with pals.

One particular Saturday he'd gotten up at five and left to go fishing with his friend Ned in Ned's boat. He promised faithfully that he'd be back in time for the party we'd been invited to. But when evening came and he hadn't returned, I found myself getting angrier by the minute.

Gerry's mother came over to babysit and calmed me down some, but my anger grew. I didn't like the way Gerry disappeared for hours and hours. I even thought about walking out with Andrea just to give him a good scare when he came home.

Darkness fell and it grew late. I knew there'd be no party for us now. My mother-in-law stayed and we made pot after pot of coffee. Gerry's mother made some phone calls, but no one had seen Gerry and Ned. I didn't worry until Gerry's mother told me that my husband couldn't swim.

That awful fear I knew so well began gripping me, twisting my stomach into a knot. Gerry's mother said all we could do was pray. I'd never been a strong believer. I'd attended church, but not regularly. I said I had no right to ask help from Someone I'd spared so little time for, but she said that didn't matter. God was always there when we needed *Him* most. All we had to do was pray and have faith.

We knelt together by the kitchen table. We prayed and prayed. I found words I never knew I had inside me, phrases I hadn't uttered since childhood. The long night dragged on slowly. By now we knew some terrible accident must have happened. Gerry's mother fell asleep with her head on the table, but I dared not sleep; I had to keep praying.

When dawn broke people went out in boats searching for Gerry and Ned. Before long, we heard they'd found Ned along the coast, and the boat had drifted ashore after it had capsized. There was no sign of Gerry yet. Still, my newfound faith didn't waver. I kept praying. I knew they'd find him, and at last they did. He was stranded on a small sandbar. They brought him in cold and shivering, suffering from exposure. He could barely speak. But he was in my arms again, safe. God had answered my prayers.

"I was drowning," Gerry told me afterwards. "I was going down for the third time. I couldn't see anything except the waves. And, you know what? It was okay, just like going to sleep. I didn't want to struggle anymore. Then I heard this voice say, 'Hang on, Gerry, don't go to sleep, hang on,' and the next thing I knew I was washed onto this sandbar."

God knew. He didn't fail me in my hour of need. And it came to me then about fear. How I'd been scared when Gerry was in the army, then on those high-voltage wires. I thought for sure he'd be safe here in his hometown, but fear is everywhere. There's no place to hide from it—except in the Lord. He is our only refuge, and our strength. I know that now. My new faith has reshaped my life.

—D.M., Canada

I knelt in the small hospital chapel and tried to pray, but couldn't. My heartache was so great that I could not even form a simple prayer in my mind. Never before had I known such despair.

My fourteen-month-old daughter was very, very ill. She had a high fever, a brilliant red rash on a third of her body, and she moaned with pain whenever she was touched. She had already spent four agonizing days in the hospital, but the doctors didn't know what the problem was. My happy, energetic little Maria had been too sick to drink, eat, or even look at anyone for five days. It already seemed like an eternity since I had seen her laugh and play, I had known many troubles in my life. Would I have to accept losing my only child too?

I sat in that chapel, alone and confused. Why was this happening? I had been praying and praying for the past few days that Maria would get well, but she hadn't. Then I remembered something that I'd read in my Bible years ago—that with just a tiny bit of faith, you can command a mountain to move from one spot to another, and it will move. All you have to do is believe.

Suddenly my mind was clear. God would heal Maria—if only I would believe! So I prayed as never before. I asked God for the strength to accept His will, whatever it was. And I put my little girl's life completely in His hands. I left the chapel feeling very close to God, positive that He had been listening.

Shortly after midnight on the same day, Maria accepted a bottle for the first time in five days. What a thrill it was to see her drink that milk! I cried with joy, for I knew without a doubt that God had heard my plea and that He would make her well again.

That afternoon I prayed that I might see Maria play with a toy again. It was breaking my heart to see her just lying in the big, steel hospital crib, never responding. The next morning a nurse put Maria in a tiny wheelchair and we went to the toy room. I showed Maria one toy after another, praying for some reaction. Finally I selected a little Ferris wheel that played music as it went around. She watched for several minutes and then reached out and pushed the wheel! Once again I was overjoyed, and I thanked God with all my heart.

That day the doctors learned that Maria had a rare disease which, in some cases, could cause damage to the heart. I was told that over the next nine months Maria would need to be examined periodically by a cardiologist. The possibility of heart complications was frightening, naturally, but I knew what I had to do— trust in God.

Slowly but surely, Maria got better, and she was able to leave the hospital after thirteen days. She is two years old now. She's happy, healthy, and more energetic than most children. Just two weeks ago she visited the cardiologist for the last time. Her heart is perfect and there is no longer any danger of complications.

I thank God every day for healing my precious daughter. And when she is older, I will have a beautiful example of God's love to tell her about: how He worked a miracle for her, a desperately ill child, and for her mother, who had nothing but faith.

—N.P., Illinois

My marriage started out as a typical 1960s marriage. My husband and I were much too young, and the babies came right away. The old saying about "kids having kids" really applied to us. Both my husband and I had a hard time adjusting to being parents and making a living for ourselves. Right after we got married my parents moved across the country, leaving me to fend for myself completely. Having only my husband's family for comfort proved to be a lonely thing for me, as I never fit in too well with them. So there I was, just living from day to day, working and taking care of my babies.

My husband soon bored of this lifestyle. He looked up his old drinking buddies and started hanging out with them. I never knew when he would be coming home or if he was—many dinners were put into the garbage after being on the stove for too many hours. The kids hardly knew their dad, and much too much money was being wasted in bars—money we could have used to pay bills.

Then the fights began. They were always the same—me

yelling and crying and my husband storming out the front door. I couldn't believe that we were the same two people who were so loving and caring just a couple of years ago. In my heart I knew that I still loved my husband, but I also knew we just couldn't live this way.

It was then that I started going to church again after not having attended for many years. The kids and I would go while my husband slept off his Saturday night. The kids loved church and looked forward to dressing up and going each Sunday. I don't think I really listened or took the things the minister was saying too seriously until one Sunday when he spoke on the power of prayer. He told us that it didn't make any difference if we were in church or at home or wherever, just as long as we opened up our hearts.

Soon after this my little girl got really sick with a kidney infection. The bills mounted up and so did my fear. One night while at her bedside, the pressures got the best of me. I just dropped to my knees and prayed my heart out. Crying and praying aloud, I stayed there for hours until I could no longer stand the pain in my legs.

As I started to rise, I felt a hand on my shoulder, helping me up. There was my husband with tears rolling down his cheeks. Together we prayed and cried and just held each other. Afterward we talked like we never had before and renewed our love. To this day I believe that if he hadn't come in and seen me like that, our lives would never have changed.

My daughter recovered and grew into a beautiful woman. My marriage did a complete turnaround and I found true happiness. We will be married twenty-three years this year and plan to be for many more. After all, we have the first six years to do over again.

The power of prayer has made a big difference in our lives. I thank God every day for the happiness I found in Him and my family and husband.

—J.P., South Dakota

Christmas was less than a week away. We had no presents under the tree, and the prospects of very many showing up were slim. I had quit my minimum-wage job in June, and my husband was on a two-week holiday layoff. I couldn't find any way to earn some money, so finally we borrowed two hundred dollars, just to help out some. It went mostly for gifts to exchange at holiday get-togethers with my husband's family and mine. I got our three children one toy and one article of clothing each. They were spoiled by getting so many presents in past Christmases when I was working, and I was afraid that they would be terribly disappointed.

I had to leave it in God's hands. "Dear Lord," I prayed, "please let the children understand. Let it be enough. I realize others have nothing for Christmas, and I don't want anything for myself—just let my children have a good Christmas. Let me teach them what Christmas is really all about." I turned it over to God and tried to stop worrying about it.

That Sunday, just before Christmas, the phone rang. It was my sister-in-law, whom I usually didn't get along with. She asked me to meet her at the laundromat with my Christmas list and no children. When I got there, I found out that she intended to play Santa

Claus so that my children could have a good Christmas. I was so touched by her generosity and kindness that tears came to my eyes.

When Christmas Eve came, my children were treated to a wonderful surprise. It looked like my sister-in-law had bought out the store. All three children got sleeping bags. My teenage daughter got lots of jewelry and some clothes. The boys got toy cars, teddy bears, snow boots, and other toys. And she even had gifts for my husband and me, including a bottle of my favorite perfume!

God answered my prayers by sending us His own Santa Claus in the form of my dear, sweet sister-in-law. I'm so grateful to them both for the wonderful Christmas they gave my family, but the gifts I treasure the most are not the material ones. My children were given an important and beautiful lesson about sharing with others, and I was given the gift of a close relationship with my sister-in-law, one I won't ever question or take for granted again. I hope we can carry the spirit of that Christmas with us throughout the year and through all the Christmases ahead.

—C.S., Illinois

I was having a difficult pregnancy with my second child. My kidneys were failing and I was readmitted to the hospital. My doctor hoped to postpone the delivery until the ultrasound showed the baby weighed five pounds, so there'd be fewer complications after she was born.

Every day I was in the hospital I had two ultrasounds and lab work done. Three days after I was admitted, my kidneys had failed enough that I was told I'd have to give birth the next morning, and the doctor told me she might not live because my baby was being delivered prematurely.

Tears burned down my cheeks. I thought about everything I'd done to stop this from happening. I was staying with my sister's family while my husband finished moving to Iowa for his new job. My sister-in-law was staying with my husband and son, since I could no longer care for him. I'd watched my diet and followed my doctor's orders.

My family put us on their church's prayer chains. *So what*, I thought. *Where's God now?* I believed in God, but prayer was for things like world peace, not one baby. I felt guilty for not carrying my baby to term. I felt guilty for not being with my son. I felt guilty for intruding on my sister's family and not being with my husband to help set up our new home.

Although my daughter did spend a lot of time in the newborn intensive care unit, she had a higher birth weight and was stronger than many babies born prematurely. "I can't explain it medically," the doctor said, "but there were a lot of people praying."

—G.K., Nebraska

I was raised by a strict father and mother who observed Sunday in the way of the old Puritans. It was "God's day" to them, a day devoted solely to spiritual discipline and cleansing of the soul. After I went away to college, I began to depart from their ways. Finally I became almost a nonbeliever in God. This was a low, bitter blow to my father and mother.

It was even harder for my parents when, after I married, my husband and I didn't send our small daughter to Sunday school or go to church with her. So my mother began coming by every Sunday and taking my daughter to Sunday school. *Oh, well,* I thought, *she likes going, and certainly she isn't learning anything that will harm her there.*

When my daughter was four, she became dangerously ill with pneumonia. One horrible night, after she had been placed in the intensive-care unit of the hospital, she turned her pitiful face to me and whispered hoarsely, "I want Granny." I was stunned and crushed by my daughter's rejection of me. Then she added, "I want her so she can talk with Jesus for me." I hung my head and cried. My mother was in California, over three thousand miles away, vacationing. I couldn't take her place to "talk with Jesus" because I no longer believed in Him.

That night passed slowly, and with each hour my daughter's breathing grew more labored. Every few minutes or so my little one would open her eyes and look around the room. I knew she was looking for Mother, but there was nothing I could do. I had already called her and she was on her way home. But time was fast running out for my daughter.

Around midnight the doctor came by and checked on her. After he had listened to her chest, he glanced up at me with tears in his eyes and said, "I've done all I can. I'm sorry." I guess he was trying to prepare me for the inevitable.

As soon as the door closed behind the doctor, I dropped to my knees beside the bed. I would not, could not, give up without a fight. Words flooded past my lips. "God, please help my daughter," I prayed. "She's so little and so very, very good. She's never hurt anyone or any living thing. If someone must die, let it be me."

The happiest moment of my life came the next day when my daughter opened her eyes and said, "I want a drink."

Later, an astounded doctor admitted, "There is healing in faith."

I thought Mother would be surprised when I told her I had "talked with Jesus" in her place and He had answered my prayer. But she wasn't. Instead, she smiled and said, "God watches over the nonbelievers as well as the believers. He sees what's in our hearts and pays little or no attention to what our foolish mouths are saying. God loves us always, no matter what we say or do."

I truly believe that God's never-ending love for all His children is the best miracle of them all. I get down on my knees every day and thank God for saving my daughter and for showing me the way back home.

—A.C., Tennessee

The last three years were a struggle. My husband was laid off from the steel mill after twenty-four years. Soon his unemployment ran out, so our financial situation was at its worst. We had raised a large family and all of our children were married or on their own, except for our youngest son, who was nineteen. We mortgaged our home, borrowed money to survive, and then put our house up for sale. Then my husband was forced to retire early, and the pension check wasn't even half of what his salary had been.

The Lord sustained us through our tough times, but then another blow was struck. Our youngest son got mixed up with drugs and alcohol. We had suspected something was wrong, but could never pin it down. The whole family was concerned, and we tried to get help for him, but his personality had changed drastically and he denied his problems.

Things got steadily worse. He would be gone for days at a time, didn't pay his bills, and eventually alienated himself from the family. All we could do was pray that he wouldn't get hurt or hurt someone else.

One night, after our son had been gone for three days and nights, I was so worried and frantic, I cried out to God. "You take him, Lord," I begged. "You gave him to us to care for and we can't help him anymore. I give him back to You. Do what You wish with him, and I will accept Your will. Only You can save him." I found myself crying uncontrollably. Then a great feeling of peace came over me, like a weight was lifted from me, I was able to sleep for the first time in days.

The next morning our son was found by the township police, sleeping in his car, not far from home. He was charged with possession of drugs and underage consumption of alcohol. I was devastated at first, but then I began to see that my plea had been answered. It was the beginning of a new life for him.

He had lost his job, and his car was repossessed. He was fined and ordered into rehabilitation for twenty-eight days. When he came out of the hospital, he was a new person.

The Lord had taken over and my son found God again. He is now in an aftercare program, has a new job, and is well on his way to a new life.

I praise God every day and thank Him for bringing my son back to me. My faith in God held me together and kept me strong.

—P.R., Pennsylvania

I was twenty-four years old, and my husband and I had split up again for the fourth time. I knew that it was finally over for good and I had no choice but to relocate and start a new life with my four-year-old daughter.

I was pretty immature about a lot of things, and now I was suddenly forced to grow up. I would have to be responsible not only for myself, but for my daughter, and I was very frightened.

With the help of my mother, I rented a two-bedroom house and hired a babysitter for my daughter so I could work. I was only making minimum wage and had to rely on that to get along. My husband refused to help, and my mother had her own bills to worry about. After paying my rent, utilities, and babysitter, I never had much money left except a few dollars for gas to get back and forth to work.

I was in a new town and didn't have any friends. I was afraid of how we would survive. I started having trouble sleeping since I was so worried, and I started drinking. At first I only drank enough to go to sleep, but then I started to need more. I became more dependent on the alcohol to shut out my problems.

Eventually I became so dependent on it that I couldn't pay my bills and missed a lot of work. My boss had a long talk with me about my drinking, and after that, I only drank on the weekends when I could sleep in. But even then I consumed too much and still didn't pay my utility bills. My water and electricity were shut off.

Instead of quitting the bottle, I bought candles for lights and borrowed water to bathe in. I wouldn't eat so that at least my daughter wouldn't go hungry. I'd lost so much weight, but I still couldn't give up drinking.

My mother threatened to take my daughter away from me, so I began to hide my drinking from her. Instead of drinking at home where there were empty bottles as evidence, I started going to the local bars and taking my little girl with me.

My moods came out when I drank. Sometimes I would be happy, other times sad, and too many times, angry. I began picking fights and soon became known as the town bully. My daughter witnessed many fights, and they always left her with nightmares. Finally, one night I picked on the wrong person and took a hard beating right in front of my daughter. She was trying to come to my defense, screaming for someone to help her mama.

The police arrested me and put me in jail. My mother came to pick up my daughter and told the police to leave me there so I would sober up and think about what I was doing to us both.

As I sobered up, the whole picture of what happened became all too clear. While I sat in that dingy cell, I prayed to God to help me. I was hungover and smelled of stale liquor. I was so afraid that I'd surely lost my little girl. I knew then that I was the only one who could get my life back in order. But I also knew that I needed help. I began to sob uncontrollably and prayed to God even harder.

All of a sudden, the stench of liquor was gone and there was a strange light feeling in my heart. It was as if someone had opened a locked door and I was allowed to enter.

I was only held in jail for the weekend, and when I finally got out, I felt like a new person.

With God's help, I quit drinking and things began to get better. I got a divorce and remarried a good man. He knows about my past and loves me in spite of it. I have never touched another drop. I know that my faith in God gave me the strength and the courage to help me cure myself.

—D.S., Missouri

On a cold afternoon one week before Christmas, my husband and I left the hospital in numb silence. Everyone at the hospital insisted on us going home so we could put up a tree and get some needed sleep.

My husband's mom was in the last stages of cancer, and it seemed to have spread throughout her body in a matter of weeks. We kept asking God over and over to spare this beautiful woman, but her condition only got worse. Why did He have to take her at Christmas, her favorite time of the whole year?

Helen had attended night college, earned her degree, and held a fine position where she worked. But there was more to her than what she accomplished in her lifetime. She had a deep faith that went beyond any I had ever known in a person, and she had a quiet kind of peace about her that you could feel. Although she never pushed her faith onto my husband and me, we seemed to sense her love of God, and that's how we began to turn to Him, especially now.

After we arrived at a department store in search of an artificial tree, we felt even more depressed. Looking all around us, we saw people rushing about, wearing robotlike expressions across their faces. The whole thought of Christmas left me confused—I felt that I had lost its meaning.

We left there without a tree. As we drove home, I kept my eyes open for a "Trees for Sale" sign, but the trees were either sold out or too skimpy.

Just as we were nearing the outer limits of the city and were about to give up, we spotted a sign which read "Boy Scout Trees for Sale." We pulled up beside the lot and saw the most comforting sight I'd ever seen. Scouts and their leaders were standing around an open fire singing Christmas carols, and all around them were big fat Christmas trees!

At that moment we forgot our pain and got out of the car to join these wonderful people. They offered us hot cocoa and a place to stand before the fire. As my husband hunted for the right tree, I stood next to the den mothers and scout masters and began singing Christmas carols with them. Tears were streaming down my face. For the first time in my life I felt the true presence of God and what Christmas was really all about.

After we agreed upon a tree, the scout salesman refused to charge us the original price and insisted on a smaller amount. He told us, "After all, it's Christmas." We thanked him, grateful that we could share the true spirit of Christmas with him.

As we headed home, I realized I was asking too much from God to let Helen live. So instead I asked Him to please just let my husband and me be with her when she departed and to help us overcome our loss after she was gone.

That same night, after we trimmed the tree with our children, we received word that we should get over to the hospital right away. When we went in Helen's room, we sensed the end was very near. Her fragile body was blue and her breathing was painfully labored. Each time our tears came, we'd leave the room to quietly release them, and then return to keep a close vigil beside her.

Suddenly a look of peace came over her face. She looked at my husband and whispered, "I love you." Those were the last words she ever spoke. Then the room became very warm and Helen's eyes opened wide and she looked up and smiled a very peaceful smile. And then she was gone. But God's presence seemed to linger. I silently thanked Him for letting us have our last precious moments with Helen. I felt that He was telling us, "I'll take very good care of her."

—R.S., Tennessee

I had left home and traveled sixty miles to attend a treatment center for people who live with the problem of alcoholism. My spirits were low and life no longer seemed to hold any promise. My family had been shattered by alcoholism. I had lost my self-esteem, and I was rapidly losing everything else I valued.

This center made arrangements with a local convent to provide room and board for women receiving treatment. Although they charged us for this service, the nuns provided us with much more. It was balm to sore hearts to be surrounded by loving women who gave of themselves and shared their strength with us.

They had set aside a large room for us containing old-fashioned beds with curtains that we could pull for privacy, and when we returned from the treatment center every afternoon full of new insights and sometimes full of pain, we often collapsed in these sanctuaries. Soon, though, we found ourselves pulling the curtains back to comfort each other and even laugh together.

Living in a dormitory room with four other women was a new experience for me, and the friendship we shared was as nourishing as the delicious home-cooked meals the nuns provided. With our bodies well fed, we began to pay attention to the hunger in our souls. We started attending mass with the nuns before supper each evening. All of us knew that somewhere along the way we had deserted God, and most of us were sure He had deserted us—or had at least lost interest in us.

One evening at mass as we began singing a hymn, I heard a voice speaking behind me. It frightened me because I was in the last pew, and I knew there was no one behind me. But there was a voice speaking to me! The words were repeated, and in a state of numbness, I kept repeating them to myself without any understanding of what was being said.

When mass ended, instead of joining my friends for supper, I hurried back to our room. Grabbing pen and paper, I wrote down the words before I forgot them. Finally, I was able to read them over and understand.

I had been so afraid of everything. Afraid that I'd lost my husband, afraid of the future, afraid to the point of paralysis. But that ended as I read the words: "Do you think I would give you less than you need?"

How could I have been so blind as to think that God didn't know I really didn't trust Him to take care of me? In this simple question was the answer to all that was frightening me. Perhaps I wouldn't have everything I wanted, but did I really think that my Lord would give me less than I needed? I was flooded with warmth and wrapped in His secure love. Here was His promise. All I had to do was trust Him.

Since that time, my trust has wavered and I have known times of fear, but I always return to that evening when God asked me, "Do you think I would give you less than you need?" and I am once again filled with strength and faith.

—S.R.A., Nebraska

My body ached with pain. My mind was filled with the misery of the doctor's last words: "You know this is a terminal illness, and you should be in a hospital where we could make you more comfortable." I pulled air painfully into my constricted lungs and felt the familiar tears rush to my eyes. It had been hard enough learning to struggle and live with the pain, but dying? I could manage the pain—but not death! How could I ever bear to leave my fatherless children when they had already lost so much?

It had been five years since I had brought my son and daughter to live with my parents, a move made necessary by the gradual crippling of my body by "skin" arthritis. I never knew when I would wake up from sleep or try to stand up after sitting a while and find myself unable to move. Painful joints would have swollen to the point of no use. Hours would pass till I could work them free or stand the pain of struggling to my feet.

My parents were wonderful. They loved me and adored their grandchildren. Mother took care of us all, and Dad saw that we had the little luxuries that made life enjoyable. They would continue to care for my children when I died.

But deep in my heart, I knew no one could love my children the way I did. My parents were good people, but they were getting old and set in their ways, and my kids needed a lot of patience and understanding, with room to grow and find their way. They needed the love only I could give them.

I had long dreamed of moving back into a place of my own where the children and I could live in our own style. When my daughter turned fourteen, she insisted she was old enough to take care of her ten-year-old brother and me and wanted us to be our own small family again. She was too young to understand my fear of the disease that ruled my life. And now I was facing death from this ugly disease called scleroderma that had crippled my extremities and was now crippling my internal organs.

It was three A.M. The house was quiet, the streets dark and eerie. I stared through the window in despair as pain gnawed at my body, each breath sheer torture. Then the words poured from my mouth, twisted in agony. Oh, how I prayed! I prayed to God from the depths of my heart and soul. I prayed for strength. I prayed for the right to live long enough to see my children grown and settled. "Please, God, I know you can answer my prayers!" I said aloud. And when I stopped, exhausted with the effort, the silence was broken by the words: "Then live as if you believe I will answer them."

Shock hit me. I looked around but saw nothing, no one. I felt goose bumps rise on my arms and a shiver course up and down my spine. Then it was quiet again, with no sound but a distant car. But I *had* heard it! I had heard those words of divine encouragement.

Gradually a warmth and peace spread over me—and also excitement! I was going to live. I was going to have my children in a place of our own. Everything was going to be all right for us— because I believed.

Over my parents' objections and fears, I moved ahead in faith. My kids and I returned to the little seacoast town that had once been our home, and the three of us pulled together as a family to succeed in this great venture in faith. It wasn't easy, but we were happy. We thanked God for each passing day and for the miracle of my disease going into remission.

Years have passed. I never asked God to heal me—He didn't. But all that I prayed for, I received. I still live. I have strength to endure the pain and the crippling. And I have the joy of seeing my two children grown and settled in loving homes with children of their own. Truly, my life has been a miracle of faith fulfilled.

Doctors say my surge of faith provided the ideal internal climate for renewed strength to combat this incurable disease. I say God answered my prayers.

—D.L., Florida

I'd only been married for three months when we got word that my husband's company would be transferring him out of the country. So we packed up all our belongings and made the long trip, leaving behind the city I had spent my whole life in. When we arrived in our new home, I took one look at it and felt like catching the next plane out.

We'd been there only two weeks and everything seemed to go wrong. Our car was stolen, our house was broken into, and my diamond necklace was taken as well. My husband had proposed the night he gave me that necklace. *That's the last straw,* I thought to myself, and I broke down and cried for days. The world that I'd thought was so beautiful had been destroyed before my eyes. I became so bitter that I took it out on everyone, especially on my husband. It got to the point that every day when he returned from work, I'd snap at him for anything he said or did. In short, I made his life miserable.

One day when I was out walking, I found a small church down the road from our house that I'd never noticed before. I walked hesitantly up the steps and peeked in the window. I hadn't been to church since I was a child. Sensing another presence, I turned around to find a little man standing there. He asked me if I would like to take a look inside. I paused for a moment, then said, "Yes, I'd like that very much."

I sat in one of the pews, gazing at the crucifix, and after a couple of minutes I broke down and couldn't stop crying. The man came over, sat down beside me, and asked what in the world could be wrong. After I'd calmed down, I told him everything, from leaving the city I loved and missed, to the disaster I was sure I'd made out of a once-beautiful marriage. We must have talked for three hours, and after our conversation I felt more alive than ever.

I ran home, cleaned our house till it was spotless, and fixed my husband the first hot meal he'd had in two weeks. He was happily surprised when he came home that day, but he never once asked me what had happened to bring about my change, and I'm not sure he ever will. I couldn't explain it if I tried. You see, I've been going to that same church for nearly two years now, and not once have I seen the little man I spoke to that day. I've even asked the pastor and the people who frequent the church about him, but no one seems to have any idea who he could be.

I thank that man, wherever he is, for putting my faith back in myself, my husband, and especially my Lord. I keep hearing over and over one thing that he said to me that day: "If you've lost faith in your family and friends and your Lord, then why should you expect them to have faith in you?"

I'll always remember those words, because almost two months to the day after I heard them, our car was found. My necklace—well, maybe someday I'll get that back. But at least my faith was restored in the one person I thought had forgotten me— my precious God.

—M.B., Florida

For years, everything in my life was wonderful. I had a fine husband, two children, and a home I dearly loved. I saw no reason for religion or prayer in my life, or the lives of my family. But things didn't stay wonderful.

Several years ago my husband lost his job and was unable to find another. We had to give up our house and move into a small two-bedroom apartment. With great difficulty, we tried to survive on savings and help from relatives. Struggling to pay bills and maintain a household, I became an angry, unhappy woman. I ranted and raved against the company that fired my husband, and I blamed him for all our troubles. I often told him, "If you had been more ambitious and gone to college, this wouldn't have happened!"

Eventually, he gave up looking for work. Some days he didn't get out of bed until late afternoon. Then he would have to listen to me yell about how difficult things were for me. The children stayed away, playing at friends' homes as long as possible, and they would often ask to stay overnight at a neighbor's.

One evening, I saw my daughter kneeling by a window. When I asked what she was doing, she said she was praying for our family. "I'm praying that Daddy will find a job and you won't be so mad anymore." I was stunned. I had never stopped to think how much my outbursts had hurt her. Then she said something that I'll never forget. "Jenny's family laughs a lot and her father doesn't have a job, either. They go to church and pray together, so I asked her mother to teach me how to pray."

Jenny's family had a strong religious background to rally them in times of trouble. Lacking in my family was the stability a religious background can bring. I looked into my daughter's eyes and knew that through her, God was telling me it was time for religion and prayer to become focal points in our lives. That night, for the first time in many years, I prayed, "Please, God, bring our family back together."

Soon we started attending church regularly and our family life strengthened. We prayed together and discussed our problems with each other. I began to feel that somehow everything would work out; I actually found myself smiling and singing again. My children were no longer afraid to bring their friends home to play, and my new outlook encouraged my husband and gave him confidence to look for and eventually find another job. A strong faith in God holds my family together now, helping us through good and bad times. And nothing will ever change my mind about the power of a little girl's prayer.

—K.L.N., California

The letter from my mother was very disturbing. My Aunt Elsie, with whom Mother had gone to live soon after Dad died, had fallen and broken her hip. "Things look very bad," Mother wrote. "Elsie is in a coma and the doctors are afraid that she might not pull through."

My first thought was one of panic: *What will happen to Mother if Aunt Elsie dies?* I'd been so happy that their living arrangement had turned out for the best, not only for the two women, now in their eighties, but for me as well. Mother had no income of her own beyond the small monthly rental fee she received from the house she and Dad had owned and a stipend from Social Security. Aunt Elsie had hated living alone after Uncle Ed died and had begun asking Mother to move in with her almost immediately after Dad passed away.

I was an only child and I felt a special concern for my mother that was in part purely selfish. Although I loved her very much, I was burdened by the thought that if ever she needed a home, it would be up to me to provide it. Now it seemed the time might have come when that possibility was about to become a fact.

But I couldn't see any way that my husband and I could take Mother in to live with us now. John was out of a job, and we were struggling to hang on to our first home on just my small salary. Then, too, our house was in the mountains where we were without inside plumbing in the winter when the long pipeline to the well below the hill couldn't be kept from freezing. It was no place to bring an eighty-year-old woman with arthritis.

Besides, things weren't going so well between John and me right then. His unemployment made him irritable at times and even led to his drinking more than was good for him. I couldn't let Mother see how bad things were with us, both financially and emotionally. She was always so proud of how well I managed, and I knew the present situation would hurt her.

But where could she go, except to come to us? She didn't need a nursing home, even if there'd been money for one. She couldn't live alone in her big old house, even if her tenants moved out, and there was no live-in help available in that small town four hundred miles away from where John and I lived.

With John's moods and his difficulties in dealing with the un-worthiness he felt from being out of work, I couldn't talk it over with him and add another burden to his shoulders. This had been a particularly bad day, with another interview ending in a turndown because John was "overqualified." After a dinner eaten in heavy silence, I was almost glad to see my husband put on his coat and leave for the village bar a quarter of a mile away.

Left alone, I kept going over and over in my mind the problem my mother's situation presented.

There was an old pump organ in the house, left to us by the previous owners. On my last visit home, when Mother had moved her furniture and things to an upstairs room so she could rent the rest of the house, I brought back with me the old hymnals I'd loved as a child so I could play my favorite hymns on the organ. I had often found peace sitting there by the hour, playing the old songs and even singing the words. So it was natural that in my troubled state on this evening, I turned again to the organ and the old hymns.

Sitting on the old swivel stool, I leafed through one of the books. When I found hymns that seemed to reflect my emotions, I played them and sometimes I sang the verses: "Be not dismayed what-e're betide. God will take care of you," and "Just when I need Him most, Jesus is near." All the while, an unspoken prayer repeated itself over and over in my mind: *Dear God, please take care of Aunt Elsie and of all of us. You know how scared I am about this.*

A great peace began to fill my heart. When I had played the last hymn, my mind was at rest and I went up to bed, feeling that all my troubles were safely in God's hands and that He would, indeed, take care of us all.

A few days later another letter came from my mother. "Aunt Elsie rallied and is doing well," she wrote. "At ten o'clock on Friday night, she came out of the coma and the doctors say she will be all right. She'll have to be in a wheelchair, of course, but she can come home next week. Thank God, we can still be together and help one another."

I laid the letter on the table, and the memory of Friday night came back to me. I remembered that I'd looked up at the clock as I'd put the hymnals away and closed the cover of the organ. It was just nine o'clock. But back in the central time zone where Aunt Elsie was coming out of her coma, it was ten o'clock.

The two sisters had a few more good years together, and when the time did come when Mother needed to live with us, both John and I were ready to welcome her to a better house and a happier time of our lives. God understood that we needed those years to grow into the maturity that enabled us to handle that responsibility when it came.

—C.H., Colorado

Christmas in Indiana was an especially hard time for our family during my childhood. My father worked for the railroad, and he would always get laid off a month before Christmas. My mother was a strong Christian woman who always believed God would take care of us.

The Christmas I was sixteen was a difficult one. My brother was overseas in the Air Force, and we were all worried about him. My mother lit a candle for him every night—Mama always believed it would help the missing person find his way back home.

Things were hard moneywise that year as well. The economy was in a mess, and so were we. If not for God's help, we would have had to forget Christmas altogether.

My mother was working as the head waitress at a restaurant, but she was making barely enough money to pay the bills. One cold winter night, four days before Christmas, a stranger came into the restaurant and he had to be seated at the bar to wait for a table. My mother talked with him for a few minutes, and later she served him his meal. When the man left, he handed Mama an envelope. "I'm a writer," he told her, "and I wrote a poem for you while I was waiting. I hope you enjoy it." My mother was very surprised, but she thanked him and put the envelope in her apron.

The next day, as she was getting ready for work, Mama found the envelope she had forgotten. In it was a beautiful poem about her—and a one-hundred-dollar bill! There was no return address on the envelope, only a name. Therefore, my mother's efforts to find the man and return the money were in vain. The poem told about my mother who was hiding a "secret" from the world, even though she smiled on the outside.

My mother never saw the man again, nor did she even mention the poem until several months later. She bought Christmas presents with the money, and she also finally found the courage to tell us her "secret."

The secret was that Mama had cancer and was going to die. She told all of us in her own special way, and we accepted it as best we could. We all read the poem and treasured it.

After many years of fighting, Mama died of cancer. I will light a candle for her every year, just as she had done for my brother and me for so many years in the past.

Oddly enough, we were never able to find out who the mysterious stranger was. Mama always thought that God had sent this man to help her along and make things easier for her in her years of suffering. I believe this also. Mama had helped many people during her lifetime, and I think God was repaying her kindness.

Christmas has a special meaning to me now because of Mama and her undying faith. I only hope my faith will be as strong as hers in the coming years.

—D.S.S., California

When my husband deserted me and our six young children, leaving us with nothing but the clothes on our backs, I made up my mind that I would not only keep my family together, but I would bring us up from absolute poverty to, at the very least, a comfortable, secure life.

After a year of my working two jobs in the city, my children and I were no better off than when I first started. It took every nickel I could earn to pay for a live-in sitter, rent, groceries, and a hundred other bills. And it hurt when my baby started calling the sitter Mama. Something had to give, and it couldn't be me. So I took a chance and rented an eighty-acre farm in a neighboring state. My family and friends thought I had lost my mind. A young woman and six small children, they claimed, could not survive in the middle of nowhere.

The farm was everything my kids and I dreamed it would be. The house leaned a little, but there was a huge old barn, chicken coops, gardens, and ponds. Our home sat high on a hill overlooking the valley, secluded and serene, and we loved it. I was able to find a job in a nearby town, and my salary was almost enough for us to get by on.

Before our first summer had come and gone, we had learned how to grow and preserve our vegetables, to care for chickens and other small animals, and even make our own soap. Soon we started selling surplus eggs, garden produce, and homemade bread and pies to supplement my income.

I felt like the luckiest woman in the world. I didn't mind getting up at three A.M. to do chores, bake pies, get the baby ready for the sitter, the older kids ready for school, and be at work by seven in the morning. I didn't even mind coming home at night and working in the gardens, baking bread, and doing our laundry on an old wringer washer. My children were happy, and for the first time in many years we were not hungry. The only thing that worried me was milk. My children needed gallons of it, but one glass a day was all I could afford.

One night, after I had finished praying, I lay awake thinking about how I could afford more milk. If we had a cow the kids would have all the milk they needed. But I didn't pray for one; God had already given us so much that it never occurred to me to ask for more. I just thought about it, and the thought was so pleasant that I soon fell asleep.

Evidently, God was listening to my thoughts. The next morning, the telephone rang and a strange voice asked, "Are you that woman with all the kids, the one that's renting the Jackson place?" I told him I was, and he said it had occurred to him that I could probably use a good cow and he just happened to have one for sale. My heart did a cartwheel, then settled into a lump. I had thirty-seven cents to my name and cows were very expensive. Holding back tears of disappointment, I explained my circumstances and thanked the man for calling. He hung up, and I went out to work in the garden.

A few minutes later, I saw a farmer leading a beautiful red cow across our pasture, a tiny red calf frolicking behind it. When the man cut across to our barn, I knew he must be the one who had called earlier—and that he must have misunderstood our conversation. I ran for the barn, hoping to catch him before he turned the cow loose.

The calf was already in a stall, and the farmer was unhitching the lead rope on the cow when I got there. He never even looked up, just said, "Better keep Red here in the barn until after the evening milking, otherwise she might not give milk tonight—"

"But," I interrupted, "I don't have any money."

"And give the calf a bottle," he continued, ignoring me. "This cow gives seven gallons of milk a day and it's real rich." With that he started back across the pasture.

"Wait!" I called after him. "How much do I owe you for the cow and calf?"

He stopped, scratched his head, and studied a cloud floating by.

"Well, can't take less than two hundred and fifty. Nope, not a penny less—when you get it." He started off again, then turned back and grinned. "I'll be back tonight to show you how to milk her."

The farmer was right. Red gave seven gallons of milk a day, enough for all of us, her calf, and four gallons left over to sell. A miracle? You bet. But more miracles were to follow.

We weaned the calf when she was six weeks old, as the farmer had instructed. Two days later, another farmer drove up with two calves on his truck; orphans, he claimed, that needed lots of love and fresh milk. He wanted twenty dollars each for them—when we got it.

By the time Red had dried up and was waiting for her next baby, we had bottle-fed the calves and sold enough surplus milk to pay for all their feed and hay. When the first calves were about nine months old, we took them to the market to sell them. That's when I discovered just how valuable our livestock really was.

Our calves brought such a price that I nearly fainted! There was enough money to pay every nickel we owed, buy more calves, and fill the barn with hay for the winter.

Within two years, we were milking five cows, feeding out more than fifty calves a year, and had expanded our operation to include fat hogs and show pigs. And then the greatest miracle of all: I was able to quit work and become a full-time mother and farmer. No, we didn't get rich, but my babies had all the milk they wanted, and I learned to believe in God's miracles.

—S.M., Oklahoma

It was one of those freak midwestern ice storms, and my job was to get my mother home after her two-week visit at my house. We didn't know the ice was coming, but about halfway through our four-hour drive, the rain turned to sleet, and then ice.

Drivers in this part of the country know what we mean when we say black ice. That means the highway turns black in certain parts—glare ice, a dangerous time to be traveling.

My husband stayed behind to go to work. In addition to my mother, our two children, ages four and two, were also passengers on this treacherous trip, buckled up in their car seats in the back.

I was driving along carefully; dusk was falling. My mother was watching the road with me, and talking on and off with the children. I left the state highway and turned off on a county road, looking for a short cut, and hoping for less traffic and maybe less ice.

A few minutes later, the car slid into the side ditch, down a rather steep incline. It happened so suddenly and I remember calling out, "Help me, God! Help me!" It wasn't a slow slide; we were bouncing along in the side ditch. I was doing my best to hang onto the steering wheel.

Then I felt a calm presence and the car slowed. I don't know how to explain it or express it, but there was a hum, an almost electric sound, and everything slowed down. Then it was as if something took hold of the front end of the car and gently brought it up out of the ditch and onto the road. I didn't drive the car up out of the ditch.

My mother felt the electric hum, felt the peaceful removal of the car from the ditch to the road, and had also been praying. She said it was an angel.

I didn't see anything, and didn't hear anything but that eerie humming noise. I know I kept my hands on the steering wheel and just let that presence take us back on the road to safety.

When we came to a stop in the road, there was no swerving or swirling as you might imagine. It was all so gentle.

Then my daughter spoke up from the backseat, "Mommy, you woke me up." I comforted her and drove us safely to my parents' home.

When we finally arrived at our destination, we told the story to my father. He said, "I was praying for you right at that time. I asked your guardian angels to watch over you."

My mother and I seldom tell the story to others anymore. If we do, they say things like, "Oh, you drove out of the ditch. You just can't remember." But we know differently. We felt it. We experienced it.

—M.E., Wisconsin

❖

How often we hear the old adage, "If March comes in like a lion, it will most certainly go out like a lamb." For folks here in southern Illinois, the month of May 1982, had a reverse pattern. It came in like a lamb and left with all the fury of a den of lions. To the south of us, rain-swollen rivers overflowed their banks, and to the north and south, as well as to the west, farmers tried desperately to plant crops in spite of soggy fields due to constant rain. Here in southern Illinois, however, we prayed that some of the showers that seemed to continually skirt us would give us even a tiny bit of moisture. Our crops withered daily in sunbaked fields.

"When the rain finally comes, we'll get a doozie of a storm like as not," an old-timer predicted, and his forecast proved true.

For weeks we'd been carrying water by hand to our rose garden in a determined effort to have the flowers in full bloom for our son Jim's graduation reception. He would be the last of our six children to don cap and gown, and this would, we prayed, be a reception he would never forget. In all likelihood he never will!

The day dawned bleak and cloudy with an oppressive humidity that stifled the air. It was Saturday, May 29, 1982, and the young folks had just returned from watching the parade in town. Last minute preparations were underway for the graduation celebration. Members of a small band had arrived and were setting up instruments and amplifiers on our roofed patio. Two large, beautifully decorated cakes waited next to a floral centerpiece on the buffet table. All was in readiness for our guests.

By two o'clock cars began to arrive, filling our driveway and an adjacent vacant lot. The graduation ceremony was over, and buffet tables overflowed with carefully prepared foods. Most of the guests had already arrived and the festivities had begun when our miracle of faith actually began to happen.

"Mom," Jim said, "stand by and greet anyone else who may still arrive, will you? I'm going into town to get Grandma. I don't like the looks of those clouds overhead, and there's a severe weather warning out for this part of the state. I know Grandma hates crowds and confusion and said she wouldn't come over today," Jim continued, "but I have this creepy feeling. I can't think about anything else. If a storm did hit, she's so unsteady with that walker of hers, she'd never get to a place of safety in time. I'd just feel a lot better if she was here with us."

Jim was right. The sky did look ominous. Hot, muggy air made clothing cling to the body, and I noticed more than one guest glance skyward with growing concern. I can remember thinking that our garden reception would in all likelihood be rained out before it had really begun. I was glad Jim had gone into town to convince Mom that she should spend the day with us. They'd always been very close, Jim and Mom. She had tried very hard not to favor any one of her grandchildren, but there had always been a deep bond between Jim and his grandmother.

How much time elapsed between Jim's exit from the reception and the onset of the storm I don't recall, but all of the borrowed picnic tables were filled with guests when suddenly the air changed and terrific winds tore away everything in sight that wasn't securely fastened down. Looking up into the angry sky, I saw a terrifying funnel cloud approaching us. Plates and cups flew everywhere, and the centerpiece and cakes landed in the top branches of a nearby cedar tree. Guests screamed and ran for the shelter of our home. Miraculously the house remained standing, but huge trees toppled over like dominoes. The cattle barn gave a sickening creak and what sounded like a dying groan, then disintegrated into a pile of splintered rubble.

When the shock had passed through the immediate area and we were able to react, many raised their eyes skyward, thankful that our lives had been spared. But our scanner alerted us to a desperate situation in the town beyond us.

Shrill sirens and a frantic voice repeated over and over: "A killer tornado has just leveled the east side of Marion. At this time it appears that a large section of the town has been devastated.

Rescue efforts are already underway. There are an unknown number of deaths and many are trapped and probably injured in the downed buildings. All qualified medical personnel please report to the closest hospital for emergency assignments."

Additional news bulletins revealed that several large shopping centers and a truck stop had gone down. Over one hundred homes were leveled and an entire apartment complex had been demolished. We were frantic. Jim and Mom had to be in that complex. Of this we were certain, yet police were not allowing anyone into the area to search for survivors without authorization or medical training. Pandemonium reigned for hours. Our guests had left hurriedly. Many had family or friends in the areas of devastation.

It was hours before Jim was able to reach us with word that he and his grandmother had survived the storm. Both were injured, but alive.

Many people within a stone's throw of them had been less fortunate. Thirteen would be found dead and two hundred injured before the final toll was in. Dead livestock lay strewn about in fields. The sight was indescribably horrifying.

When we were able to hear an account from Jim, he told of reaching his grandmother moments before the twister struck. When he realized that there was no possible escape, Jim had carried her into the bathroom, urging her to lie down in the tub. He protected her with his own body, stretching himself across her. There they escaped from the fury of the storm. Both were cut by flying glass as the sliding-glass bathtub doors shattered, and both were bruised and badly shaken as the entire building crumbled into a twisted pile of rubble. Most of the dead and injured had been in this apartment complex when the tornado struck.

One of the victims was a young woman who only hours earlier had been in Jim's graduating class.

A speaker at the ceremony had said, "It is sad to say, but this will be our last time together as a group. Never again will we see all of our classmates together." He could not have known, nor would he have wished to, how chillingly accurate his statement was.

Our hearts will ache for some time for those who must bear this terrible grief, and we will be thankful for those of us who were spared. As for myself, I am certain that had it not been for the intuitive miracle of faith that sent Jim rushing away from his reception to his grandmother's side, she would have perished.

—S.H., Illinois

I desperately wanted a little brother or sister for our daughter, who would be entering kindergarten in another two months, but my husband was dead-set against it. He adored our little daughter and argued, "Another child would mean taking away from our daughter, and I don't want her deprived of anything."

Since I couldn't persuade him that we could supply enough love and material necessities for two children, something told me to pray about it, so I did. As I began, I recalled the words of my late grandfather, who'd been the pastor of a little country church. *When you pray for rain, show some faith. Start carrying an umbrella!*

It occurred to me that we still had our daughter's old bassinet in the basement, so I cleaned it up and brought it into our bedroom. That would be my umbrella. When my husband asked what it was doing there, I told him I was thinking of maybe doing some baby-sitting after our daughter started school. He didn't say anything about it, but he was unusually quiet the rest of the evening. The next morning I woke up to see him standing by the bassinet, looking at it intently.

"What are you doing, sweetheart?" I asked.

"Just remembering how precious our daughter looked in this," he answered, "and wondering what a second one of ours would look like in there."

My miracle of faith was a son born about the same time his big sister started first grade.

—C.M., California

The Christmas of my ninth year is bittersweet in my memory—bitter with the poverty and misery of the Depression, sweet with the memory of my mother's faith and courage, and with the miracle of the sunflowers.

My father died when I was three years old, leaving my uneducated mother penniless and with four children to feed. I was vaguely aware that we were poor, but so was everyone else in our tiny town. It was not until many years later that I realized that we were experiencing utter poverty and had little hope of survival. I vividly recall meals of oatmeal without milk, of black-eyed peas picked on shares and cooked without meat, and of cardboard in my shoes and newspapers wrapped around my body under a thin coat to keep me warm.

I know now that it was a depressing and degrading time for my mother, who worked when she could at our four-room schoolhouse as a janitor, and who washed clothes at night and hung them on the line to freeze during the night and dry by day.

But she had an indomitable will and an abiding faith. We said our prayers and went to church and, after reading late into the night by lamplight, I remember, she would bow her head at the table and pray. She assured us that God would provide for us. She nursed sick neighbors, and she always seemed to have a potato or a bite to eat for each of the destitute men who came down the Santa Fe tracks across the road in endless streams, roaming and searching for work.

We never knew where the sunflowers came from that grew in the barren dirt of our half-acre yard. One day they were simply there, tiny green sprouts that grew into a towering, tangled mass of thick stalks and leathery leaves. They filled the yard except for the garden spot that my mother kept cleared. My older brother wanted to cut them down, but my mother stood on the back porch, eyes squinting in the summer sun, and forbade it.

"God's got a purpose for everything," she said. "Let them be."

They were a delight to my sisters and me. We burrowed through them and made secret hiding places where we could huddle in the stifling, green semidarkness and whisper about our dreams of growing up. Fall came, and then the most agonizing winter of my memory. The sunflower leaves turned brown and blew off and the stalks looked grotesque in the moonlight when I went outside to the privy.

Meanwhile, my mother had run into a man named Charles with whom she had worked thirty years before; he had been a dear friend who had left the area and returned. He was one day to be my stepfather, the only father I ever knew and whom I loved very much. He began coming to see my mother about once a week and always insisted on bringing groceries, so at least we began to eat better. Even though he offered, my mother refused to accept money from him; she was reluctant to marry him, too, because she didn't want to burden him with her responsibilities.

The winter set in and my brother and I scoured the fence line and the creek banks near the house for firewood. We split the wood and kept stoking the kitchen range to keep its enormous appetite satisfied. It was the only source of heat we had. We slept under mounds of blankets, but dressed, undressed, studied, and lived in the kitchen.

Just before Christmas, a howling norther hit, and the wind poured in through the siding and around the windows and doors, which we draped with old sheets and blankets. The wood we used for fuel seemed to disappear.

"We'll burn the sunflowers," my mother told us the night before Christmas Eve. "That's why God put them there."

She gathered up some newspapers and string and took them with her when we all went into the yard in the moonlight. My brother and I cut the sunflowers into stove-length pieces and my mother and sisters wrapped them with paper and tied them with string. We worked late that night and all the next morning and filled the kitchen and a small storage shed with bundles of these sunflower stalks.

The stove ate up the bundles as if they were tinder and we fed it constantly, the damper closed and the lids off for warmth. I've since decided that we would have died of carbon-monoxide poisoning if there hadn't been so much oxygen pouring in through the walls.

On Christmas morning, we raced from our beds to the kitchen to dress and my mother sat by the range, feeding it.

"Look in the parlor," she said.

We had cut a tree and decorated it with our tattered tinsel and strings of threaded popcorn and red berries. My brother had cut a star from cardboard and covered it with tinfoil from discarded cigarette packages he'd found. We each had a stocking filled with pecans and an apple and an orange. Wonder of wonders, we each had a gift—a pair of socks for me, I remember.

We went back into the kitchen, chattering away. But my brother, who was more aware of others' feelings than the rest of us, was disturbed. "We don't have anything for you, Mom," he said.

She smiled and held up one of the remaining bundles of sunflower stalks. "This is all the Christmas I need," she said.

There was a noise in the driveway, and we ran to the windows and peered out. There was Charles in a truck loaded with firewood and, we found as we ran outside, with groceries and presents for us all.

"I figure this has gone far enough," he told my mother with his quiet smile. "These are Christmas presents, so you've got to accept them."

They were married shortly after that and life suddenly changed for all of us. My stepfather had the house weatherproofed and painted, added a bedroom and a bath, a water system and a septic system, installed butane, and had the house wired for electricity. We would never again know hunger or cold or fear.

I remember that time now that my own children are grown and gone, visiting frequently with children of their own who enjoy lavish Christmases. I think of that time most often while working in my garden, the envy of my neighbors for its quantity and quality of produce. They attribute my success to knowledge and care. But I attribute it to the little patch of sunflowers that I plant each spring for the cardinals, along with a prayer of thanksgiving.

—J.A.C., Texas

In June, I was watching a special on TV. The program was called "World Ministry to Others." It was a very touching and sad program about those very poor people in Calcutta.

My heart really went out to them, but I myself am a poor person. My husband only works every other week, and his unemployment checks for the weeks he was laid off were only seventy-five dollars. Also, at that time I was trying to save up some money to start buying my children school clothes.

But after watching that program, I made a promise to myself that I was going to send fifteen dollars to them the very next day, which I did. I only had about twenty-two dollars saved, but I knew that by sharing what little I had with others I would be blessed.

For some reason, I enclosed a letter along with the money order I had gotten. In it, I explained that I understood what it was like to be poor. I told them about how I was sharing with the poor the money I had saved for my children's clothes.

Usually, I would watch a telecast like that, say to myself that I would send some money, then change my mind the next day. But it was different this time. I had to send that gift of love.

Well, about three and a half weeks later, I was still trying to save for my children's clothes, but I didn't seem to be getting anywhere. I mentioned to my husband that I still had no idea where our children would get jackets for the fall weather.

The very next morning, I noticed that there was something in the mail from the place where I'd sent my donation. Inside the envelope I saw what I thought was a receipt for the money I'd sent. But what I found was a love gift of one hundred dollars, a check made out to me to buy school clothes for my children. The letter said that they had received my letter and gift, and that they took my letter into prayer and one of the brothers was led to send me a love gift. It was done in the name of Jesus Christ, our savior.

I know in my heart that God was with me while I was watching that program and while I was writing the letter and mailing my gift. My faith is now stronger than ever. I pray that someone else will one day receive a blessing as great as mine.

—B.E.R., Georgia

I was fifteen years old that humid August night in 1968.

I was sleeping soundly in the bedroom that I shared with my sister Connie when an urgent hand shook me from my slumber. I sat up and focused my eyes on the intruder. It was my Uncle Bill. I looked at the clock: two A.M. *Why is Uncle Bill here at two in the morning?* I asked myself. *And why is he in my bedroom waking me up?*

"Patty," he said, "something has happened. Come downstairs so I can talk to you."

I slipped groggily from my bed and threw on my robe, then followed him down the stairs. The whole downstairs was ablaze with lights, and as I shuffled to the sofa to sit down, I noticed that my other uncle, Ed, was there, too, sitting in the wing chair.

Uncle Bill took both of my hands in his and spoke. "Patty, your mom and your Aunt Marge have been in a serious automobile accident." Tears streamed down his cheeks. "Honey, it's bad. They are both in surgery now. Your dad and your sister Marcia are both at the hospital. It was Marcia who answered the telephone when the call came in. Right now, that's all I can tell you. We'll just have to sit and wait."

I sat back on the sofa, stunned by the news. My mother and aunt played pinochle every other Thursday night with friends. Their little club was named the "Thursday-nighters." It was almost the only form of recreation my mother had. Raising eight children was a tiresome task, but come those special Thursdays my mother would perk up with renewed energy and cheerfulness in anticipation of enjoying an evening out with her girlfriends.

At about three-thirty, my father called and spoke with my uncle. The news was that both women were still in surgery and that things looked bad. My aunt had been driving and had failed to make a sharp curve in the road. The car had crashed head on into a telephone pole, sending my aunt, face first, into the steering wheel and my mother through the windshield and back. Although other women from the club had been on the scene within minutes, the prospects did not appear good.

In all the time since I had been told about the accident, I hadn't cried—not when my uncle first broke the news, nor when my father called to verify the seriousness of the situation. I don't know why. It all seemed so very unreal to me, and all I could think about was how I wished morning would come so that things would be better. Morning had always seemed to make things better before.

The hours dragged by slowly, as they always do when one is awaiting news, whether it's good or bad. But when morning finally did come, so did the telephone calls from frantic friends and curious acquaintances. All were stunned by the news.

By eight o'clock that morning, the rest of the children in our family had been told about our mother. My sister Connie, having been called home from a friend's house where she was spending the night, was just coming in the door when my father got back from the hospital.

I had never seen my father cry before, and then, at fifteen, I was finding it to be one of the most painful experiences of my young life. I held back my tears as my father's sobs mixed with those of my brothers and sisters and the close friends and relatives who were now beginning to gather in our living room. I hoped that my being strong would help in some way.

My father brought news that both my mother and my aunt were out of surgery and were still in serious condition. My aunt, he told us, was going to make it. She had suffered a broken jaw and foot, and had several serious lacerations. But my mother, he said, was suffering from internal injuries. She had broken her arm and her shoulder as well, and her face was badly cut. She had lost a lot of blood, had head injuries, and the outlook for her was dim.

The roomful of loved ones broke out in renewed wails of anguish and I left the room then, knowing that now was the time to speak to God.

I ran to my bedroom and flung myself across my bed. I began to think about promises I could make, ways I could bargain with God, so that He would spare my mother's life.

But I was a typical teenager of the sixties, selfish and self-centered. I was hardly the person to ask for a favor from God. I had always done chores around the house, but not much more than was asked of me. I spent my free time running around with my friends, often doing things that I knew I wasn't supposed to do and going places that were off limits. I had tried my hand at smoking and shoplifting, and had always balked at going to church with my family on Sunday. My vocabulary was full of four-letter words, very popular with my age group, but never spoken within hearing range of my parents.

So what could I offer God in return for my mother's life? I could promise to attend church services gladly every Sunday morning, and even to take communion. I could promise never to swear or to think evil thoughts again. But would He agree to the deal? What if He didn't? What if my mother died anyway?

"Dear God," I prayed aloud. "Just tell me what it is You want of me. Should I stop fighting with my sisters? Promise to become a nun? Just give me a sign and I'll do it. My dad needs my mother. My brother and sisters need her. I need her. Please don't take her away."

We waited two whole days before the call came from the hospital, informing us that my mother had been taken off the "guarded" list. She was still in Intensive Care, but she was going to live.

Right after the good news came, I decided to take a shower. As I lathered up the soap in my hands, all of the worry and tension and pain, bottled up in me for so long, finally came flooding out in loud, long sobs. I washed and I cried, I cried and I washed, letting the warm water rinse away my grief.

I began to thank God, over and over in my mind, for answering my prayers, but it wasn't until a few moments later that the full realization of how wrong and how foolish I had been to actually believe that I could bargain with God finally hit me. God had sent my family a miracle because of His love for us. There had been no need to try to strike up any bargains with Him.

Looking back, I cannot consider this a miracle that resulted from faith, but rather faith that resulted from a miracle.

—P.C., Washington

At eighteen years of age, I thought my world was perfect—at least until the day my parents calmly told me they were getting a divorce. Mama moved back to her hometown to build a new life, and my father married a widow with two sons.

Although both parents invited me to make a home with them, I somehow felt I would be happier on my own. Using all my savings as a deposit, I rented an apartment in a once-fine house that had been converted into small, cheap apartments. With the exception of one young man and me, the only inhabitants of the apartment building were senior citizens. *So what?* I thought. *Who wants neighbors dropping in all the time?* I figured the older people would be so frightened of living in such a run-down neighborhood that they would sit behind locked doors all the time.

An elderly lady lived across the hall from me, along with her two pet parakeets. Each morning, when I left the building for work, she would be standing at the top of the stairs, telling me to have a nice day. When I returned in the evening, she would once again be standing there, asking me how my day had been. I would always mumble a couple of words to her, then run into my apartment. *Who needs some old biddy snooping around?* I would think angrily. *She probably just wants someone to listen to her problems, and I've got enough of my own.* My father was so wrapped up in his new wife and family that I had only seen him twice in six months. My mother, too, was busy getting back into the swing of single life, having more dates in a week than I did in a year.

I knew Mrs. Simms, my neighbor, must have wondered at times about my lack of friends and dates. Several times, within my hearing, she told her birds about people who shut themselves off from life. *It's none of her business*, I would think. *It's my life*. Still, I refused to try to make friends with anyone, and the few friends from high school who were still inviting me to go places with them soon quit calling after I turned them down repeatedly. Night after night, I would sit in my room, reading books and watching television.

One morning, almost a year after I'd moved in, Mrs. Simms wasn't waiting at the stairs when I left for work, nor was she there when I returned. Even though I told myself good riddance, I still missed her greetings. When she didn't appear the second day or night, I told myself she must have taken the hint that I didn't want to be friendly. But when there was no sign of her on the third morning, I decided to check on her when I got home from work that evening.

When my knocks went unanswered, I finally decided to call the manager of the apartment house and have him let me into her room. While I was standing outside my door waiting for him, I listened carefully for any sounds coming from her apartment. At last I heard noises, as if someone was bumping into things. Again I pounded on the door, and this time it opened. There stood Mrs. Simms, her dress torn, her hair uncombed, and bruises on most of her face. One eye was swollen completely shut, the other partially closed.

"Mrs. Simms, what happened?" I exclaimed. "Were you robbed, or did you fall, or what?" Secretly, I was wondering if Mrs. Simms had a husband who beat her.

"I fell down the stairs," she answered, her voice quivering. "I overslept the other day and didn't want to miss telling you good-bye. I was running to catch you and misjudged the distance. A blind person has to be careful about that, you know."

I stared at her for a long moment. "You're *blind*, Mrs. Simms?" I asked dumbly.

"All my life," she answered matter-of-factly.

Suddenly my heart went out to the old woman who had tried to brighten my world, even though hers was dark. When the manager of the apartment house arrived a short while later, he insisted that Mrs. Simms be taken to the nearest hospital. When she asked me to accompany her, I said yes without hesitation. Then when the doctor told her she would have to have surgery to relieve the pressure on her eyes, I told her I would be there with her at the hospital. When I asked who she wanted me to call to tell about the accident, she replied, "Why, child, I have no one but you."

That evening, after taking care of her parakeets, I went to my own apartment, but I was unable to concentrate on anything. Two thoughts kept running through my mind: The doctor had said Mrs. Simms might not come out of the operation, and Mrs. Simms's admission that she had no one but me. Long after I'd gone to bed I was still awake. Finally, toward dawn, I knew what I needed to do, but I couldn't do it. I wanted to pray, but I didn't know how.

I got out of bed and paced back and forth in my room, regretting the fact that my parents had never been churchgoers. Suddenly I realized that Mrs. Simms would be going into surgery soon—*something* had to be done! Clearing my throat, I began to speak. "Lord, I know You're up there, and people say that You listen in times of need. Well, I'm in need now, so I want You to listen very carefully. An old woman is going into surgery in less than two hours. Her doctor says she may not make it; she's weak and she's old. He doesn't know she's all alone, Lord. But You and I do.

"I'm going to make You and Mrs. Simms a promise right now. If You'll let her live, I'll make sure she's never alone again. I'll try my best to pass on to someone else the kindness she showed me. Just let her live, Lord, and I'll learn to be the best human being I can be." Filled with a strange sense of peace, I was able to leave for the hospital, feeling better than I had since before my parents' divorce.

Mrs. Simms was just being wheeled to the operating room when I arrived. She was drowsy, but alert enough to grip my hand and whisper, "God bless you, child."

In the waiting room, I continued to talk silently to God. When the surgeon finally came out and said Mrs. Simms was fine, I meant it when I said, "Thank God!"

When Mrs. Simms was allowed to leave the hospital, she moved into my apartment at my suggestion. She began to talk of how she and her late husband had attended church before his death, and I became curious as to why she never went any more. "Well, most people don't have time to help an old lady around," she told me. "I can't get there on my own because of the traffic."

I realized then with a guilty feeling that I had never had time for Mrs. Simms until tragedy struck. The next Sunday, she and I were proudly sitting in the front row of her church. On the day of my baptism, she couldn't have been any more proud of me if she'd been my mother. She became my friend, my surrogate mother, and the person I loved most in the world.

Six years after I met Mrs. Simms, I got engaged to be married. I had written this story with the intention of mailing it before my wedding. However, in the rush of things, it was pushed into a drawer where it lay until today. Instead of being just a story now, it is my tribute to Mrs. Simms.

I was married on June 26, 1982. While on my honeymoon, I received a telegram saying that Mrs. Simms had died in her sleep in the apartment she and I shared. I can only pray now that Mrs. Simms is in Heaven, where her world is as bright as she made mine.

—D.S., Illinois

I had been badly injured in an automobile accident years ago, and the doctor told me then that I would very likely encounter complications if I were ever to get pregnant. More specifically, he thought it would be difficult for me to carry a baby full term. When we married, my husband knew how much I wanted children, but he, too, thought I should never get pregnant. But three years later, the matter was taken out of our hands when I got pregnant despite the precautions we had been taking.

Even though he was a little frightened for me, my husband was overjoyed at the news, and I was delirious. I made an appointment with my doctor as soon as I suspected that I was pregnant, but before that date came I started bleeding. I rushed to the hospital emergency room, where I was told I was probably not pregnant. They ran some tests, however, which confirmed that I was pregnant after all. The doctor said that the best thing I could do was to stay off my feet as much as possible and, if the bleeding started again, to lie flat on my back.

I was very careful, but the problem continued throughout my pregnancy. I also worried constantly. Somehow I knew that this would be the only chance I would ever have to be a mother. I needed and wanted this baby so much.

Tension and worry started taking its toll on me. I was so emotionally drained that it was starting to affect me physically. I didn't know where to turn. I felt so helpless. I needed a power stronger than my own.

Finally, no longer able to cope on my own, I turned to our Heavenly Father. I had not prayed in a long time, and I wasn't sure if I still knew how, so I started very simply. "Dear Lord," I prayed, "if You are really there and You can hear me, please let this baby be all right."

As my pregnancy progressed, I worried more and more, but I prayed more also. With each prayer, it got a little easier, until one day I realized I was making contact. It wasn't only the words I was saying, but the feelings coming from my heart that I knew God heard.

The worry and heartache became too much for me to bear, and finally I surrendered the whole thing to the Lord. I praised Him for allowing me to experience the joy of feeling my child move within me. I thanked Him just for giving me the beauty of a pregnancy. I asked only for His will to be done in my life and my baby's, and I prayed for the strength and the courage to accept it.

One day, after a very heavy rainstorm, my husband called to me from the open doorway. I went to stand by his side, and I saw the most beautiful double rainbow that I'd ever seen. It started in a puddle in the field across from our house, arched up over our front lawn, and ended in a brilliant splash of color on the north side of the lawn. I was suddenly filled with a feeling of peace and joy, and I heard a voice say, "Ease your troubled heart, child. Your baby will be born just fine."

I truly believe that I had heard the voice of the Lord, and I knew He had sent that beautiful rainbow as a sign for me.

The bleeding continued throughout the remainder of my pregnancy. I took good care of myself, and followed all of the doctor's orders, but I no longer had any fear or worry. I also continued to pray, just as I do now. Each day I praise God for the precious, healthy boy He has given me, and I thank Him for the great honor and privilege of being a mother.

Praise God for the miracle of life that we call children!

—C.W., Pennsylvania

It was early December and snow was falling lightly when I stopped at a local department store for some Christmas shopping after work.

We'd moved into our new home in a busy suburban area a few months earlier, and I'd changed jobs knowing the extra income from a higher-paying job would be a great help with the higher mortgage payments.

My husband and I had been married a few years by then. I'd moved in with him when we married. We'd always planned to sell his house and get our home.

After scrimping and saving, amid downsizing companies and a recession, we'd finally sold the house, putting the equity and most of our savings toward our new home. Money was tight. We were both driving vehicles that needed replacing years earlier.

When I left the parking lot of the department store, I took an unfamiliar exit that I thought would take me to a more direct route to our new home. I made my right turn across the road and, to my horror, turned into oncoming traffic.

Snow was coming down quickly. I was panicking. I started beeping my horn to alert the oncoming traffic that I was in the wrong lane. I steered my car onto the meridian strip that divided the traffic lanes, all the while honking.

I was now stuck straddling the meridian, beeping furiously, watching for traffic behind me in my rearview mirror, as well as traffic coming toward me.

I started praying out loud to myself as I tried vainly to get my car off the meridian and into the right lane. As headlights approached, I furiously prayed, "Our Father, who art in Heaven . . ."

As I prayed, two men appeared, one tall, blond man and another shorter, older man. I rolled down my window, still panicky and shaken, as the blond man bent down to my window.

"Just steer the car straight." He smiled at me. "We'll lift it over the curb. Easy on the gas." The other man stayed at the back of my car, poised to help.

"Okay." I breathed, still praying, but a calm coming over me. The two mortal angels lifted my car off the stretch of meridian, smiled, and waved me off as I drove on, this time in the right lane of traffic, the snow gently swirling.

I looked back at the two men in my rearview mirror. Just as suddenly as they appeared, they were gone. I'll always believe they were angels sent to answer my prayers.

—M.B.S., Minnesota

I had always considered myself a normal, average person with no unreasonable fears. I had traveled some, been over mountains and through caverns a number of times with never any qualms or anxieties. Then about ten years ago, I suddenly developed an overwhelming case of claustrophobia. I could not even go downtown among the tall buildings, much less ride in an elevator or go to a shopping mall where I couldn't see an exit. If I went into a large store, I had to keep a good view of the outside. To visit friends and relatives in the hospital was out of the question, and any business that had to be attended to was taken care of by another member of the family, unless it was on the ground floor. When friends invited me to any functions, I declined because of the fear that we might get in a closed-in area. I missed out on so many activities, but I couldn't quiet my fears.

There was prayer offered on my behalf about this condition, but for some reason there was no change.

Then in July 1979, my husband was scheduled for minor surgery. He was put on the fifth floor of the hospital. My son and our pastor and his wife went to the room with him while I remained in the lobby, ashamed that my husband needed me and that I could not bring myself to step on that elevator.

That evening, I came home very much aware that something had to be done. I talked to my husband on the phone and he said that the doctor suggested that I use the stairs up to his room, but I knew that I couldn't do that because the stairs were also enclosed.

All I could do was walk the floor and pray. Finally, I said, "God, in the morning before my husband goes to surgery, I'm going to get on that elevator and go up to his room. I know that when I step on that elevator, You will be there with me, so whatever happens is in Your hands."

A peace washed over me and I even began to look forward to morning. Early the next morning, my two daughters and I went to the hospital. The elevator came, the door opened, and without hesitation we stepped on. When the door closed, I took my daughter's arm because I was not quite sure what to expect. The elevator stopped twice before we reached the fifth floor and I was feeling great. When we reached our floor, I stepped off with tears of joy and thanksgiving.

I rode several elevators that day, and after my husband's surgery I went down to the recovery room which was underground and down a long hall. Since then, I go wherever I need to go. Occasionally, when someone mentions going to the hospital or mall or any closed-in area, for a brief second that fear returns. But I have a scripture that can combat any phobia: "For God has not given us the spirit of fear; but of power, and of love, and of a sound mind."

—R.B., Texas

For several years, I have been teaching a class in psychiatric nursing. My students and I work with patients who are thought to be "incurable" and "hopeless" cases. These patients will probably spend most of their lives locked behind the walls of a state institution.

It's a challenge for me not only to convince my student nurses that they can make a difference in their patients' lives, but also to convince the patients that they *can* change. Working with these patients has been a source of constant blessing to me, and has allowed me to experience many "miracles of faith." One instance that I particularly remember concerns a patient named Bob.

Bob was one of the youngest patients on the unit, and had withdrawn into a catatonic state. I was disturbed by this because one of my students and I had been working closely with Bob and he had seemed to be making progress. Now, when we went to see him, we found him lying flat on his back. He was holding himself very rigidly and was staring at the ceiling with wide, unblinking eyes. He looked "scared stiff"—frightened and very vulnerable.

My student also looked frightened and unsure. She didn't know how to approach Bob or what to say, so I moved closer to his bed and sat down. I didn't say anything, and Bob didn't seem to know I was there. After about five minutes of silence, I told him that I was worried about him and that I wanted to help him but felt locked out. When I asked him if he would like to talk, he didn't say a word.

Not knowing how to penetrate his wall of silence, I suggested that he answer my questions by blinking his eyes for "yes" and squeezing my hand for "no." To my surprise and delight, he blinked his eyes. Just to be sure, I asked him to squeeze my hand, which he did. We began to communicate, and I learned that Bob was indeed feeling very frightened, but he wasn't sure why. Not talking and holding himself rigid was his way to stay in control—something he thought was necessary. He also told me that he didn't want me to leave.

After we had continued in this manner for some time, I asked Bob if he would like me to pray with him. When he blinked his eyes, I said, "Lord, remove the burden of fear from Bob and re-place it with Your peace and love. Let Bob turn to You rather than withdraw into himself, and let him experience the power of Your healing in his heart, mind, and spirit." My student and I remained with Bob for a while longer, and then went about our other duties. We visited Bob's room frequently throughout the day, but his condition remained the same.

When we returned the next day, we found that Bob was back to his old self, and was walking and talking freely. As we approached him, his face broke into a big smile. He thanked us for being with him, and especially for my prayer.

I was so grateful for that experience. I knew God's power had penetrated Bob's withdrawal. God had touched Bob, but He had also touched my student and me, confirming for me the need to share God's love with the patients and students He entrusts to my care.

—V.C., Maryland

Mrs. B. was much more to me than a supervisor. During the years we worked together, we became very close friends. We shared many funny, sad, and happy experiences and talked about everything under the sun. We shared the same views on many things, from religion to how to handle a husband. Mrs. B. once remarked that listening to me sometimes sounded like a rerun of her own life, since she was over twenty years my senior.

My friend had a strong faith and spoke often of her closeness with Our Lord and how He had helped her through some trying times in her life. Her church played a big part in her life. Even though I, too, believed in God and prayer, I guess you might say my faith came and went according to the circumstances of my life.

Eventually I changed jobs, Mrs. B. retired, and we drifted apart except for an occasional phone call or greeting card. After her husband's long illness and finally his death, a visit I made to Mrs. B.'s home convinced me that she would be all right—her faith would sustain her.

There came a time in my life when I began to really feel something was missing. I was so very aware that I was unhappy about my life. I became more aware of the sins around me. The people I worked with began to look and sound differently to me. I was aware of the gossip, cursing, jealousy, deceit, and infidelity taking place all around me. I wanted out! After talking it over with my husband, I gave my notice and quit my job. It was a job that paid more than I'd ever made in my life and I'd trained hard for it, but I couldn't wait for my replacement to take over.

I loved staying home—the leisure time and just feeling free. But something was still missing. I began to pray more, and sometimes I surprised myself the way the words would just flow from my mouth, saying just what I wanted to say. But often I'd find myself wondering: *Is He there listening to me? Does He really care? Does He hear me when I pray for the guidance in my life I need so badly?*

Then one night I had a dream. In my dream, Mrs. B. and I were walking toward a vast body of water to look for something. As we stood looking out at the water, I felt disappointment wash over me because I saw nothing. I was very upset and turned to my friend, saying, "Why, there's nothing out there, nothing at all."

She smiled and turned me around in the opposite direction. Pointing out toward the water, she exclaimed, "Look, there it is, the lighthouse! *It is still there.* Look at it." And as I looked, I wondered why she was making such a big deal over a faded old lighthouse when I had expected to see so much more.

The dream remained very clear in my mind over the next few days, and because I've always felt some dreams have special meanings I wondered about it.

On Sunday morning, despite the fact that I had a dreadful cold, I got out of bed. I didn't want to miss my favorite evangelist on TV or any of the beautiful hymns before his sermon. After the first beautiful hymn, the second soloist took his place. I snapped to attention like a soldier when I heard the title of the song: "The Lighthouse."

The singer began, and as he sang the words, "Jesus is the Lighthouse," I knew the meaning of my dream: He *was* there, shining His light on me, guiding me, and I had only to turn and look in His direction—the right direction—and He would be there for me. Whatever else I had been looking for, He was all there is.

Yes, as the hymn says, "I thank God for the Lighthouse." And I thank Mrs. B. too.

—P.H., North Carolina

I wasn't surprised when I started to hemorrhage in my fifth month of pregnancy. After five miscarriages, I had learned that being pregnant doesn't always mean having a baby. For me, it meant watching the light go out of my husband's eyes as I started cramping and hemorrhaging.

Several doctors had warned me not to get pregnant. They told me there was something wrong with my uterus and I would never be able to carry a baby to term. They also told me that this pregnancy had to be the last; another miscarriage would surely kill me. So this was my last chance to give my wonderful husband a child of his own to hold.

As the ambulance rushed me to the hospital, I felt numb with despair. No baby—ever. How could I live with that? I think I still had a tiny grain of hope left until the doctor said the baby had dropped and the fetal heart tone was a very low sixty. Miscarriage was imminent and there was nothing anyone could do. In that moment, I hit rock bottom. Then I remembered the one person to whom nothing is impossible—our lord and savior, Jesus Christ.

I closed my eyes and began to pray. I didn't ask the Lord to save my baby because He knows our every need. I just thanked Him for the baby I knew was going to be born when the time was right. When I said amen, I very clearly saw a pair of hands holding a tiny baby, and suddenly I was calm. I knew Jesus was watching over my little one and I had nothing to worry about.

Later, when the doctor came back to check on me, he was surprised to find me in such good spirits and even more astounded to hear a strong fetal heart tone of one hundred and thirty. The baby was high up in the womb and stirring normally. The doctor couldn't explain it, but he delivered that miracle baby a few months later: a beautiful baby girl.

Every day since then I thank God for our precious daughter who was born through faith and God's love.

—S.M., Texas

Until about ten years ago, I'd thought my life was an exceptionally rich one. Although I'd never married, I was blessed through my two sisters with a large, wonderful family of nieces and nephews, their friends, spouses, and, eventually, their children.

In addition, there were my own friends, going back to my high-school days, for I had a gift of keeping the friends I'd made. My job, which I enjoyed, my volunteer work, my music, and my church completed the joyfulness of my life. I thanked God every day for it.

Then, at fifty-three, I began to go blind. At first it didn't seem like much—an occasional odd, sharp pain in my left eye, headaches, a little blurred vision. But all too soon, I learned it was serious; my left retina was detaching.

An operation, which had seemed successful, had to be redone within the year. Within three years I had five operations. I prayed; my friends and the members of my church prayed. But the eye got worse.

Then my right eye began to go the way of the left. I became frightened. I wept. I prayed harder. There were more operations. I could no longer drive to church or write my old friends. I could barely keep my job.

And my music, my biggest solace, was nearly gone too. I could hardly see the notes to play my piano.

There were more operations. I hoped; I prayed. Others prayed with me. I thanked God for my many friends, but I also cried in despair, "Why me?"

Then came the last operation. It had to work, or I would be blind forever. If it failed, I felt my life would be over.

My pastor came to me the evening before the operation. As we were talking, I asked him, "Does God really answer? Look how I've prayed, how we've all prayed. This is my last chance, and I'm running out of faith. I don't think I can pray anymore."

"Maybe we've been saying the wrong prayers," he suggested. "Let's try another one. Let's try Christ's last prayer, and let's place our trust in His will."

"Father," he prayed, "if it be Thy will, take this cup from her. Nevertheless, not our will, but Thine be done. Amen."

"Amen," I echoed.

The operation failed; I was blind. Totally, permanently blind. I grieved. For a while, I was bitter. Everything—my job, my music—was gone, it seemed. My pastor visited me often and encouraged me to wait on God's will. We prayed together and my faith held up, even if it seemed, at times, feeble.

One day my pastor brought a man with him. He was new to the church and lived near me. This man, before he retired, had taught piano by ear. He said he'd teach me just to keep his hand in. I almost didn't accept his offer; I really didn't think I could learn. Sheer boredom was my motive for saying yes.

But in no time I was playing the piano again. Oh, they were simple tunes, but I was learning to play them in every key. It was a whole new ball game, it was fun, and I was learning to do things I'd never done before.

Encouraged by that success, I started to learn Braille. Friends taped parts of my favorite magazines and dropped by often to deliver them. On my own, I discovered talking books. The woman next door began driving me to church and, through me, became a member.

I lost my sight, finally, just after Easter 1980. This past Easter, I played for the church services for the first time in years. With my newfound skills, I was able to transpose the solo into a key our new tenor could handle, something I had not been able to do when I could see.

My life now is more exciting than it ever was before. Every day I pray my new prayer, "Father, not my will, but Thine, be done." And every day brings something new.

—N.I., California

It was a bitter March day and snowing heavily. I was visiting my cousin, Charlotte, in her new house in a still-uncompleted development on the water's edge. Afternoon visits were something quite new for me; I had worked as a registered professional nurse ever since I'd completed my training. Just a week before, I had put aside my white uniform to await the birth of my first baby in another three months.

Charlotte and I sipped our hot tea. I was watching the snowstorm through the dining-room window when I saw the man. He was walking out of the icy bay, naked from the waist up, his skin reddened and raw. He was approaching my cousin's house, stumbling as he walked, looking as if he was about to collapse. I could see his teeth chattering.

"There's something wrong, Charlotte," I said to my cousin. "Let me have my coat. I think he needs help!"

Charlotte looked frightened. "What if he's drunk, or an escaped lunatic or something? There's nobody else around here to hear us if we shout for help. Don't go out," she pleaded.

"I've handled worse than this in the emergency room," I told her. "The man is sick or something. I can't just *sit* here!"

Reluctantly she handed me my coat. "Don't forget that you're six months pregnant. Don't lift him or anything."

I ran toward the man and reached him just as he collapsed in the backyard. I shouted to Charlotte, who was shivering in the doorway, "Come out here and help me. If you don't I'll drag him into your garage by myself!" She realized that I meant business and hurried out. Somehow we managed to pull the now-unconscious man into the garage.

"He's probably in shock," I said. "Get some blankets and put some water up to boil. Bring some liquor, and your portable heater, too. And hurry!"

Charlotte ran into the house. The "head nurse" tone in my voice was stronger than her apprehension. I elevated the man's feet so that the blood could return to his head. His pulse was weak and his flesh was ice cold. Within five minutes I had wrapped him in three blankets, the garage was warming up, and I had a conscious patient! He sipped slowly at the tea Charlotte had made. Finally he spoke. "God bless you," he whispered.

I reassured him while Charlotte called an ambulance. In a weak voice, he told me his name was John Riley. He had been fishing, but the stormy winter sea was too strong for his rowboat. The small craft collapsed. He'd kicked off most of his clothes in an attempt to swim to shore. The lights in Charlotte's windows had shone through the storm and he prayed that there would be help for him. I lifted a glass of brandy to his lips.

The ambulance arrived soon after, but before leaving for the hospital, the driver took my name and address. After calming a very distressed Charlotte, I left for my own home.

That evening my telephone rang. A woman's voice, heavy with emotion, said, "I am John Riley's mother. Are you the person who saved his life this afternoon?"

"I did what I could," I replied. "How is he?"

"He has pneumonia, but the doctors think he'll live. God bless you, my dear, for being there and helping him."

"Why on earth was he fishing on a day like this?" I asked.

"He has six children," his mother explained, "and there's never enough money for food. I told him it was foolish, but—"

My eyes filled with tears. What *If I hadn't been there?* I thought. Charlotte probably would have been too frightened to have done more than call the police. He might have been dead before the ambulance arrived.

"John told me you're expecting a baby," the woman went on. "Are you Catholic?"

"No," I replied, not understanding.

"Well, then," Mrs. Riley said, "I'm going to make a novena for you and your unborn baby—so that he'll be a healthy, strong child. You saved *my* son's life; the least I can do is pray for *your* child!"

I kept in touch with the nurses at the hospital, and soon learned that John Riley made a speedy and complete recovery. But, unfortunately, things didn't go as well for me. In my seventh month I went into premature labor.

My child was born quickly—a three-pound boy closer in size to a mouse than a baby. The doctors weren't optimistic. My tiny son was moved to a specially equipped nursery for premature babies. I prayed fervently for his life.

John Riley's mother prayed, too. We had spoken to each other often while John was hospitalized. In addition to her nine-week novena, she burned a candle in the church every morning for my little Michael. Somehow, Michael pulled through and slowly grew stronger.

The miracle of his survival never ceases to amaze me. There was every reason for him not to live: His lungs and heart were not fully developed. His body was not ready to leave mine—not ready to function on its own. As a nurse, I understand that. But I know, too, that a miracle of faith was what made him survive. God helped me because I had helped John Riley, who might have died had I not been there that snowy day in March.

—M.K., New York

My husband and I each attended Sunday school and church regularly as children, but somehow after we were married it was easy to find excuses for not attending. We lived on a farm, and morning chores for our dairy herd continued well into the time the Sunday-morning services started. The same thing was true at night—milking was never finished until the evening services were half over. As a result, we just drifted away from going to church. I suppose we could have been called nonparticipating believers. We did see to it that our six children attended Sunday school, were baptized as Protestants, and took part in church-sponsored youth activities. They made up in religious activity for what we lacked.

When our eldest daughter went away to college, she brought home any number of boyfriends. We accepted them all with no thought of her ever getting serious about any of them. So it came as a great shock when she asked us one day what we would think of her becoming a Catholic. One of her boyfriends was of that religion, and he would not convert to hers. My answer to her was that it really didn't matter to me which church she attended as long as she did attend. After all, hopefully we are all going to the same place, and more than one road leads to that heavenly destination. My childhood faith was liberal enough to accept other religions.

However, my husband became furious and blew up. No child of his was going to join another church, he said, or even worse, marry a man of a different faith. When tempers had cooled down, my daughter went back to school, but continued to visit us on Sundays, always bringing the same young man.

One day after they had visited with us for an hour or so, she spoke up quietly. "Paul and I want to get married," she said. Her father stormed out the door in a rage. She would be disinherited if she married Paul, he said (we didn't have much of an inheritance to leave, anyway), but worse yet he would have nothing to do with her for the rest of her life. I prayed that his attitude would change. I didn't want to lose my daughter, but I didn't want to lose my husband, either.

When a letter came a few days later from our daughter with wedding plans and an invitation for us to take part in them, my husband insisted that his word was law and that none of our family could take any part in it. We would go into a period of mourning for her as if she were dead. I prayed to God that my husband would change his mind and see that different kinds of believers could all be good people, and that we would become a family once again. It seemed that the more I prayed, the more stubborn he became, and I could not get him to change his mind. It was tearing our family apart.

A month after the wedding, my daughter and son-in-law came home to visit us. My husband happened to be in the house when they drove up. By the time I went to open the front door, he had disappeared out the back door. They visited us off and on during the first year. Each time they came he would leave, although he didn't fuss about the rest of us seeing her. "Thank You, God, for softening his heart," I prayed. "Help him to see that he is hurting himself more than her, and help him make his way back into her life."

However, my husband was very stubborn and always managed to be somewhere else when she came. I was a bundle of nerves, wanting to see her; yet not wanting her to come because it upset him so much. When she wrote letters, he wouldn't read them or listen if I tried to read them aloud. He would get up and walk away. It got so I'd just leave them on the table where he couldn't help but see them, and although he wouldn't read them in my presence I knew he was secretly reading them. I would fold the paper a certain way and come back later to find it folded differently. He really did love his daughter.

Years went by. Babies came—first a little girl, then a second, and the next year a third, with no grandfatherly love given to any of them. I never prayed so hard as I did before each baby came. "Make their grandfather able to experience the joy those babies could bring him," I'd ask God. I'm not a nagger, so I said nothing to my husband to try to change his mind, but I prayed constantly. The other children were all friendly with their sister, but they had to see her secretly—no family Christmas parties, no summer picnics, no mentioning of her name in conversations with their father.

Eventually our youngest son went off to college. When it was time for him to come home for the summer, my husband was busy with field work, so I had to drive to the college town to bring him home. When we got home, I saw a car in the yard with an out-of-state license plate. There also were three little girls picking dandelions in the yard. My heart jumped to my mouth. My son and I went into the house. There in the living room my husband was having a great visit with our daughter and her husband. I never found out what happened. But it was an answer to my prayers that I wasn't home when they arrived unannounced, because my husband had to come in from the field when he saw a car in the yard.

That was the first of many happy visits. Eventually he visited them in their own home.

Yes, God does answer prayers, even for those who do not attend church. Sometimes it may take Him years, but in the end He is there. When I see my granddaughters, I thank God that they had a chance to get to know their grandpa before he died recently. They had three years to make happy memories of him. What a shame it couldn't have been ten.

—M.P., Wisconsin

E veryone has known the worry of not knowing where the money will come from to pay off debts. I recently carried a terrible burden—only it wasn't a conventional debt I was worried about. Mine was from gambling.

You see, I had a weakness for playing slot machines, and anyone who has ever put a quarter in the slot and pulled the arm of that bandit knows how you can get hooked. Well, I got to the point where it was not just five or ten dollars I was losing. I would go out on Friday night after getting paid and blow my whole paycheck. I'd walk away empty-handed with a terrible feeling of guilt, without a penny to live on the whole next week.

I had some friends in my small town, so I was able to get gasoline and cigarettes and other items on credit until my next payday. I ate bologna sandwiches for lunch, so I got by.

But when payday came again, the fever struck and I was totally helpless and at the mercy of those machines. They seemed to hypnotize me. I could not help myself as I fed roll after roll of quarters into their greedy little bellies. Of course I would hit a jackpot every now and then, but I only put it right back in. I could not stop.

So you can understand my anguish when I woke up one morning penniless and started getting calls from all the people I owed, asking for their money. I had run up a bill of three hundred and fifty dollars before I even realized it! And where was I going to get the money?

Then I remembered the people I used to work for and how good they'd been to me, loaning me money when I needed it. And I had always paid them back. Sylvia, the store owner's wife, and I had gotten very close when I worked for them and I remembered she had told me if I ever needed help to just call her. People often say things like that. But how could I go to her and say I needed three hundred and fifty dollars? But I thought it was worth a try, and it was the only chance I had to correct my mistake.

I gathered up all the courage I could muster and went to talk to Sylvia, praying on the way. I asked God to let her see fit to loan me the money. God had answered my small requests in the past, but this seemed like too much to ask. I didn't know whether to tell her the truth—that I needed the money to pay off gambling debts—or to lie to her, saying that I needed money for something like medical expenses or car repairs. I just didn't know what to do.

As I was driving to see her, I passed a church that had one of those marquees out front where they put up different little sayings to make you think. And do you know what it said that day? These are the very words: *"Honesty is the first step toward the solution to any problem."* It was a message straight from God! At that moment I knew that God was on my side and that I should tell Sylvia the truth.

You can imagine how humble I felt as I discussed my problem with Sylvia. Of course she was upset that I had let my weakness get the better of me, but she didn't scold me or preach to me. She knew I had gone through enough anguish.

Then she told me something remarkable. She said that she'd had a strange feeling for the past few days that someone she cared about was in trouble. She didn't know who it was or what the trouble was, but she went to church and prayed about it, and told God that she was willing to help that person if she could. And sure enough, here I was asking for help. Needless to say, Sylvia gave me the money. But then another thing bothered me: How was I going to pay her back? She told me not to worry—to just send her what I could.

Then another miracle happened. Sylvia asked me if I would consider working part-time at her store, since she and her husband were getting into their busy season and needed some extra help. I was thrilled! That way I would be able to pay her back out of the money I made part-time, and still have my regular paycheck to live on. God not only answered my prayer about the money, but he also gave me a way to repay it!

I was able to pay back the money within about four months, and to this day I have not pulled another slot-machine handle. Don't think I haven't been tempted, though. But I ask God to give me strength against that weakness so I won't find myself in that same situation again. And God has answered my prayers once more.

I thank Him every day for His goodness and for giving me such a wonderful friend. My faith in God was renewed, and also my faith in my fellowman. And if any of my friends ever get "slot-machine fever," I hope I'll be there to help them through their time of despair.

—D.C., Georgia

Our only child, a son we named Jon, was born to Dan and me late in our life. From the time he could crawl, Jon resisted the rules and values that were so much a part of our lives. As he grew older, he constantly reminded us that our ideas were old-fashioned and obsolete. Hot tempered and defiant—and more than a little spoiled—he insisted that he wanted to make his own rules, wanted to do his own thing. At seventeen, he became involved in drugs and dropped out of school.

Heartbroken, we observed the troubled and angry look in his eyes, his surly behavior and unkempt appearance. We were filled with pain as we watched our strong, healthy son become pale and dissipated by drugs.

We tried to help him, tried to reason with him, but, like most parents, we did not know how to cope with someone dependent on drugs. We tried professional help, but Jon refused to cooperate. We made mistakes—many of them—and some of them hurt Jon. Often, we were filled with remorse about the mess we'd made as parents.

Shortly after he had dropped out of school, he ran away. Dan and I were frantic. We lived in fear and suspense for several weeks until Jon finally contacted us. He stated that he was doing fine, that he wanted to do his own thing. He warned us that if we made him come back, he would only take off again. Realizing he meant what he said, we just expressed our love and concern and told him we would be here if he ever needed us.

Dan and I waited for months, hoping and praying for his safety. On sleepless nights—and there were many of them—we paced the floor, crying and wondering.

Then one night, I was awakened from a deep sleep by the jarring ring of the telephone.

When I lifted the receiver, I recognized Jon's voice immediately. "I'm at the bus depot. Will you come and get me?"

At first, I was overwhelmed with gratitude. Then fear gripped me. "Are you all right?" I asked quickly.

"I'm fine, Mom," he assured me.

When I first caught sight of the longhaired boy who stood waiting outside the depot as Dan and I drove up, I winced. He was so thin, so frail. Then I held out my arms and he ran eagerly into them. Unashamed of our tears, the three of us stood there, in the middle of the night, hugging and kissing.

When we arrived home, we were all too excited to sleep. We sat around the table and talked. Jon told us he was off drugs. He talked enthusiastically about going back to school.

Then he told us how lonely and depressed he had been, how his friends had betrayed him for a handful of pills. He had found new friends, only to have the same thing happen again. He had wandered from one meaningless job to another, sometimes quitting after several paychecks, sometimes getting fired because he was in no condition to work.

He told us that one night after receiving his pay for a week's work, he had gone to a bar, where he had met two guys. They had several drinks together, then the guys had invited Jon to their place. Instead, they had taken him out into the country and knocked him unconscious. He had been robbed and tossed into a ditch.

When he regained consciousness, he was chilled to the bone and he didn't have the least idea where he was. Filled with despair, he started to walk down the road in the darkness. The area was deserted except for a farmer's yard light in the far distance. Then as he walked, he saw a cross on the horizon. Later, he discovered it was attached to a little country church, but at that moment, it was a beacon for him.

Focusing on the cross, he started walking toward it. As he walked, he recalled scriptures from the Bible he had heard as a child, about how the Lord is near to those who are discouraged; how He saves those who have lost all hope; how He gives the lost new strength and guidance and leads them down the right path.

"All the drugs and the running did not help me to find myself," Jon said. "I discovered I couldn't run far enough or fast enough."

Later, in my bedroom, I knelt down on my knees and thanked God for bringing our son back to us, for helping him win his private battle with himself.

His return was truly a miracle of faith. God had been with him all the time.

—H.C.E., Tennessee

When my father passed away, my mother went into a deep depression, and I didn't want her living alone. Even though she was only fifty-three, she'd depended on Dad to conduct any and all business and banking. She'd never learned to drive, and now I needed to take her shopping and run errands. I begged her to move in with me. I felt she didn't need to be by herself. She was hesitant because she was afraid of invading my space.

I finally talked her into renting her house and moving in with me on a trial basis. If it didn't work out, she could always move back home or into an apartment where there was no grass to mow. By renting the house it wouldn't seem so permanent. After we got her all settled in her new room, I said, "Tomorrow we'll go to church and give thanks for the first Sunday the two of us are together."

She smiled as she went to bed. In the morning, when I knocked on her door to tell her it was time to get ready, she said she didn't feel like getting up just then and would pass on church that morning. Thinking she was tired from the excitement of moving, I let it drop.

When I came home later, I told her what a good sermon she missed. The next Sunday there was another excuse for her not to attend church with me. This went on for several Sundays until she started complaining that I was gone all the time—every Sunday morning—and didn't want to spend any free time with her. Other than going to work, I was with her all day.

She finally told me she'd lost her faith because her husband had been taken from her at a young age and now she was alone, just when they should've been enjoying life together. I tried to explain that she had me, even if I was a poor substitute, and that both God and I loved her.

When I came home one Sunday, she was on the front step. She'd fallen when she went to get the paper. She said, "If you'd been here instead of going to church, I wouldn't have fallen." She hobbled to the car with my help, and I took her to the emergency room. The doctor told her she was lucky, it was only a sprained ankle and he bandaged it. On the way home I told her it wasn't because I'd gone to church that she'd fallen, it was because she'd stayed home. If she'd gone with me, she wouldn't have slipped on the step.

During the week, she seemed to be getting around fine, but on Sunday she took another turn for the worse and needed me to run errands before services. If I'd done everything she wanted I would've been late for devotions. This went on for quite a while, until it was time for our revival and annual dinner on the grounds. Everyone was to bring a covered dish. There would be people from all over. The whole congregation looked forward to this yearly event. People who also experienced losing a loved one and going through hardships would be there.

It took me all week to convince my mother to even consider going. When Sunday came, she was ready with her famous pecan pie. When we came home I could tell she'd definitely enjoyed the services and the dinner. Everyone raved about her pie. All week she talked about how the preacher had moved her.

The next Sunday she went to church with me, no excuses this time. When the preacher asked if anyone wanted to dedicate to God, she got up, went to the altar, repented for backsliding, and asked for forgiveness.

She is now one of the most devout members of the congregation. She doesn't miss a service unless she's really sick in bed. It's been over two years since Dad passed away, and there is a gentleman around Mom's age who has been asking her out for coffee after devotions. He seems like a nice guy. His wife passed away a few years ago, so he can identify with Mom. She told me she was going to meet him next Sunday. I hope this leads to happiness for them, as they both deserve peace. I'm sure Dad would approve of Mom getting on with her life.

—C.P., Arkansas

Ron was on unemployment when we found out that I was pregnant. We had been married almost four years, and for the first three and a half years had wanted a baby very much. But then Ron got laid off and we quickly ran out of money.

I was ecstatic, but Ron was worried. We were broke, and Ron couldn't find a job anywhere. We applied for Medicaid, but we were just over the limit (five dollars over).

Well, Ron couldn't take it, so he left. Before he did, he asked me, "How will we pay the hospital bill? Or feed the baby and put clothes on his back?" I couldn't answer him, and I couldn't stop him, so I let him go.

At first I think I was in shock. I didn't know what to do. I thought God had deserted me. How could He do this to me and my unborn child? How could He let this happen? Well, Mom and Dad took me in and persuaded me to try again for medical assistance. I did get it this time, along with a photocopy of the warrant they made me put out on Ron for child support. Oh, I was so bitter! Everything I loved was gone. Where was the love and help I so desperately needed from God?

Well, time went on. I thought of my baby nestled inside of me and I was comforted. I loved her (I decided the baby had to be a girl—I couldn't bring up a boy without a father). Yes, I loved her very much. And then one night as I lay in bed crying, lost and alone, she moved for the first time! Just a little at first, then it seemed as if she rolled over and cuddled up to me. It was so wonderful, but there was no one to tell it to. I had to tell someone, so I told God all about it. Of course He already knew, but it felt so good to talk to Him again.

I heard very little from Ron. But I would talk to God and ask Him to bring Ron back to the baby and me.

My due date was May 17th. Ron showed up at my parents' house on the evening of May 17th and said, "The baby is going to come tonight." I told him not to be silly—babies never come on their due dates. But he insisted, so I let him in. We talked a lot and finally it was getting late. I was tired, and I told him he would have to leave. He said, "The baby is coming, and I'm staying." So I went to bed and let him stay.

At 12:27 A.M., the labor pains started. I went downstairs where I found Ron asleep on the couch. I had taken a course in Lamaze, so I did my breathing exercises and timed my contractions for a few hours. In between, I prayed that Ron had come back for good and that the baby would be healthy and strong.

After a while, I woke up Ron and Mom, and called my sister who was going to drive me to the hospital (she was also my Lamaze coach). We took off for the hospital—my sister, Ron, and I. After I was admitted, everything happened so fast that it is a blur in my memory: a haze of huffs, puffs, pants, and prayers.

And then there she was at 6:56 A.M.—my little girl, Bonnie Ellen, all pink and wiggly.

That evening, Ron came to visit and to feed our baby girl, and I knew he was back to stay. His look of love shone down upon the little elf who looked so much like him. And God and I both knew. . . .

It's been sixteen months since that day in that room of hope and love. I have my little girl and the man I love so much. Every night I lie in bed and talk to God. I tell Him the day's events, and thank Him again and again for the three loves of my life: Ron, Bonnie, and Him.

—R.D., Ohio

Little Billy was born July 15th after ten full months of pregnancy. A grim doctor—a specialist whom I had never seen before—came to my room to tell me Billy "had a few problems." That turned out to be a euphemism, meaning he was totally physically and mentally disabled. I cried at first—his being blind seemed to strike me the hardest. I pulled myself together in time for my husband's first visit to the hospital.

That was the only time I cried. Bill and I were much too busy just keeping little Billy alive to waste much time on self-pity. He would stop breathing and turn blue. He needed special bottles flown in from Boston just to feed him. He had seizures. He couldn't even cry properly, so he had to be watched carefully to make sure he was all right.

I began to feel like I lived at the hospital. If the baby wasn't in the emergency room with some new illness, he was getting casts changed to correct turned bones in his feet and ankles. Or he was at his almost weekly checkup.

By the end of the first exhausting year, Billy weighed only fifteen pounds and needed the first of several operations. A doctor from New York was flown to California to close the cleft in his soft palate. The operation was a success, and I thought things would get easier. They did for a while.

Three months later we were told Billy needed another operation. The bones in his ankles and hips needed to be "turned" so he could continue to grow without being in great pain.

Bill and I were about at the end of our resources—emotional, physical, and financial. Bill was only a laborer in a steel mill, and

I was accidentally pregnant again and very ill. And little Billy, at only eighteen pounds, was hardly ready for another operation.

Not knowing where to turn, we finally went to the elders of our church. We expected little more than moral support, but, at this point, even that was desperately needed. When they heard our plight, the bishop suggested a "laying on of hands," healing as it is spoken of in the Bible. While my faith did not stretch to include such a thing as faith healing, I went along with my husband and set the date for the next Sunday—the day before the operation.

That Friday, Billy went to the hospital for X-rays. The surgeon needed them for consultation with several other doctors.

Sunday came, and after the sermon the elders, the Bishop, Bill, myself, and little Billy went into a side room. There, the elders applied olive oil as commanded in the Bible, and we bowed our heads to pray.

Suddenly the room became very warm, and a bright light filled it. It was so bright my closed eyelids glowed red. It was over as quickly as it came. All that was left was a deep sense of peace and calm when we opened our eyes.

There was no apparent change in Billy, but we went home feeling better than we had in months. The next day I took him to the hospital for admission. We were sent to the X-ray department for one last set of pictures. We waited for them and then took them back to the surgeon.

A few minutes later, the doctor appeared and told me that there had been a mistake; I had been given the wrong X-rays and he wanted to have them done again. The second set was met with mutterings, a long delay, and then several doctors' looking at the X-rays, examining Billy, and looking at the X-rays again.

I was then informed that there would be no operation. Between Friday and Monday, the "casts" had done their work. For the first time, turned bones had been reversed without surgery. We had to stay for measurements and photographs for an article in a medical journal, but Billy came home with me that day.

I would like to tell you that Billy was completely healed at that time—that he runs and plays and goes to school with his sister—but I can't. I do not know God's reasons for Billy's afflictions. I do know God was there when we needed Him most, that He has been there, mitigating illness and easing burdens which at one time would have been too much to bear. I also know my faith now stretches to include faith healing. It stretches to include a very personal, loving God. And it stretches to include believing in miracles.

—M.M., California

When I went to the doctor's office for my yearly routine checkup, I expected to hear the usual "Everything is just fine." However, the doctor detected a lump on my breast, and he suggested that we keep a close watch on this and check in a few months to see whether it had enlarged.

When I arrived home and told my husband, he could see no reason in waiting that long to have a surgeon check it. After all, one of the ways to combat cancer is to discover it early.

When the surgeon examined me, he was very frank in telling me what to expect when I went into the hospital for the operation. The lump would be removed and a biopsy of the tissue would be done immediately to determine whether it was malignant. He told me that if the tissue was found to be malignant, immediate radical surgery would be performed. In plain words: the removal of my breast!

The operation was scheduled for about a week later. During this time, I walked around almost in a daze. There were no thoughts that I could command which would ease my uncertainty and my apprehension. No one could say calmly, "Everything will be all right. You have nothing to worry about." More than anything I wanted to hear this. It wasn't that I was afraid to go to the hospital. I had had plenty of experience being a patient. I had been there for an operation due to a tubal pregnancy and for the delivery of three normal babies. This would not be the same.

The night before the operation, a fellow church member who was recovering from a colostomy at the same hospital came to my room to visit me. That was kind of her, but not even she was able to alleviate my uneasy feelings.

When the anesthetist came to see me, I told him of my fears and that I did not want to be aware of all that would go on the next morning. He understood and assured me that I would not be awake. He prescribed a sleeping pill for that night. Again in the morning I was brought a sleeping pill, and then a shot was given preparatory to going to the operating room.

Although I was quiet and apparently sleeping, I was not at ease. My mind was still fretting about the outcome. Still, no one could say to me, "Everything is going to be all right." At the same time, there seemed to be nothing I could tell myself to put my mind at ease.

Just as real panic set in and I was thinking: *What is going to happen? How am I going to cope with this?* I heard very distinctly the words: "Trust in the Lord." At last the heavy load was lifted from my mind as I was wheeled down the hall to the elevator and then to the operating room.

Where did the words come from? I will never be quite sure. This was a Baptist hospital, and a devotional was given over the intercom every morning. These words could have come from there. The drugs might have had something to do with it. I know I was not dreaming, because I was quite aware of what was happening from the time I heard the words and then was pushed down the corridor and into the operating room. It was only after I arrived in the operating room that I was completely out.

Thank God the operation turned out fine. There was no malignancy and perhaps all my worry was for naught.

A few weeks later when I attended church, I met one of the older, faithful members in the hall. She inquired about my health and then said, "We were praying for you."

Without hesitation, I answered, "I know you were"—for this must have been where the words I heard had originated from: the prayer circle which was always held whenever anyone was undergoing an operation or was in trouble and in need of prayer.

If anyone questions the power of prayer, I can always cite this experience as concrete evidence of its power. And the scripture Isaiah 26:4 is one closest to me:

"Trust in the Lord God always, for in the Lord Jehovah is your everlasting strength."

—L.J.W., Missouri

When I was in the eighth grade at St. Thomas School, I won first prize for a composition that I wrote about the missions in China. The prize was a beautiful crystal rosary. I loved that rosary and carried it with me always. Little did I realize what an important part it would later play in saving my life.

When I was fifteen, my parents divorced. My whole life seemed to turn upside down and I felt very insecure. I lost all interest in school. I began to run around with a fast, loose group of kids with completely different values from the ones I had been taught. I began to drink and smoke pot. I fought constantly with my mother, and when she threatened to "straighten me out" I ran away from home.

For three months I lived on the streets, staying with one friend and then another. When my so-called friends ran out, I was left to fend for myself. One chilly autumn night I had no place to sleep. One of my friends gave me the key to his van and told me that I could sleep in it for the night. I was cold, so I turned the heater on. That was the last I remember until I awoke in a hospital.

I found out later that a young priest from a nearby church was coming home from the YMCA where he taught an evening class. He spotted something sparkling and glittering under the streetlight. He stepped over to the curb and out of the gutter picked up the crystal rosary that had fallen from my shoulder bag. When he picked up the rosary, he noticed that the motor of the van was running and a strong smell of carbon monoxide was coming from it. He saw me unconscious in the front seat. A faulty muffler was pouring fumes into the closed van. He called the emergency squad and they took me to the hospital.

A nurse went through my belongings and found my home telephone number. She notified my mother, who came at once to the hospital.

When I was released, my mother and I both went to see the young priest who saved my life. We wanted to thank him. He was very kind and suggested to Mother that we both get special counseling to help us adjust to the changes in our life.

It was not easy for my mother or me to make the necessary adjustments, but with the help of God we did find a way. We also found a new mother-daughter relationship that is beautiful. It was truly a miracle of faith that not only saved my life, but helped Mother and me get through the bad times and realize that life is indeed beautiful.

—Anonymous

In 1979, my husband and I started a small business—one in which he had ten years of experience. We both worked long, hard hours, and our two oldest sons, aged seven and ten at the time, worked right along with us. The first year was very hard on the family. It seemed like we were always tense, tired all the time, and watching every penny. Our lives had become all work and no play.

After nearly eighteen months of this, we were able to hire three employees. I limited my duties to bookkeeping and could concentrate once again on raising my three young sons and taking care of my husband. We began doing business out of our own home, and it was easier for me to do both of my jobs.

In spite of the new employees we had hired, my husband could not seem to spend any less time at work. He would not let go—he only had faith in his own ability to make things work, not anyone else's. As the business grew more successful, he began to become more and more involved in his work. He insisted on running the whole show, and was determined that his contribution to the business be the greatest. He began to look like a man on the verge of a nervous breakdown. He talked only of work during every waking moment.

Worst of all, our family life was going downhill fast—again. My husband had no patience with me or our children. He expected me to do *my* job—running the household—perfectly. This, he said, would make it easier for him to do *his* job. He wanted to be waited on hand and foot: wonderful meals, a neat house, well-behaved children. His reasoning was that I was home all day while he worked long and hard for his family. I was there to be sure he was cheerfully given anything he needed. He proved he loved his family by working so hard, he said.

Life was becoming impossible. I loved my husband and couldn't stand to see him become such a work-driven monster. I feared I would soon become a widow; he couldn't keep up the pace much longer. I began to pray for comfort, knowing that God loved us, but things steadily got worse. The final straw came when I made a small bookkeeping mistake. My husband really blew up at me and told me that if I was one of his employees he'd fire me.

The argument that followed turned out to be a blessing in disguise. My husband finally realized what was happening to our family, and I was able to talk him into buying a small used camper for us to use on weekends.

The day before we were to leave on our first weekend trip, my husband took the children to a nearby creek to find fishing bait. This was the first time in over two years that he spent time alone with our children.

A few hours after they'd gone, the phone rang. My husband was being taken to the hospital by ambulance—he had broken his leg. He had damaged his leg muscles so severely that it was two weeks before the doctors could put a cast on—and it would be six to nine months before he'd be able to walk again.

I realized later that my husband's accident was God's way of answering my prayers to help my family. My husband was doing nothing risky when he broke his leg. He was walking on smooth ground at the time; there was nothing for him to trip over. All he remembers is walking along and blacking out.

My husband now looks ten years younger. Color has returned to his face, and he is rested and relaxed for the first time in years. Now he has the time to be aware of just how much his family loves him.

My husband had been on the road to having a heart attack, and I couldn't slow him down. God not only slowed him down, He wised him up. My husband was forced to become dependent on others—just temporarily. As a result, he has learned that his employees can and will do what is necessary to keep the business running smoothly.

The pain our family felt while my husband was working so hard has been replaced by a feeling of love and an inner peace in all of us. God *does* work in mysterious ways, and we will never stop being grateful that He does.

—P.H., Pennsylvania

When I was twenty-three, I was transferred almost five hundred miles from home by the company I worked for. I had no friends or relatives there and I was very lonely, but before long I met a man and fell very much in love with him. He was alone in town, too, and also very lonely. Although we both knew it was wrong, we soon became lovers.

A few months later, I found I was pregnant. We discussed abortion, but we both had very strong feelings against it. We didn't know what to do, since neither of us was really ready for marriage. Finally, we decided to live together and just see how it would work out.

Things went from bad to worse. We fought constantly over everything and our burden of guilt was overwhelming. One evening, after a particularly bad fight, I walked out and drove away to cool off. I hadn't been a regular churchgoer in years, but somehow, when I found myself passing a church, I couldn't resist the impulse to stop. The door was unlocked, and I went inside.

What peace and quiet there seemed to be! I immediately felt calmer. Words just seemed to form on my lips from nowhere. I prayed for knowledge of my own heart. Even as I prayed, I realized how much I loved this man. Then I asked God to let him realize his love for me or to give him the courage to admit he didn't love me and leave. I knew that would mean having my child alone, but that seemed better than the hell we were living in.

When I returned home, we spent the night in silence. The next day I left on a business trip, fully expecting him to be gone when I returned. On my second night away, I walked into my motel room and found him there! In a moment, we were in each other's arms, talking together and crying.

He told me how much he loved me, and then handed me a little box. Inside it was a plain gold wedding band. It wasn't fancy, but it was (and still is) the most beautiful ring I have ever seen. A few days later we were married.

That was three years ago. We are a happy couple now, with a fine daughter. Every Sunday we attend church, and with God's help, we will always remain a happy family.

I am sure God was listening to me that day in church and that He answered my prayer.

—R.P., Texas

It's easy to have faith when all is going well, but when heartache strikes we are forced to search our hearts and see the sad truth about ourselves. My husband and I had our troubles in the past; however, when he joined Alcoholics Anonymous I carried high hopes for his recovery from alcoholism, and thus for the success of our marriage. He obtained a good job and took on many financial obligations in an attempt to prove to himself that he was capable of handling responsibility. I'm sure he felt this would insure his sobriety.

But suddenly he was gone—a thousand miles away, to his home state, deserting his two children and me, and leaving me with a huge stack of bills. I had a part-time job, but hardly enough income for groceries, let alone the support of two small children. When I heard from him, he was drinking again, living with his parents, with no job in sight. I went into panic, then depression. I would pray mechanically, but somehow the words that came out of my mouth were not being felt in my heart. Self-pity engulfed me, accompanied by constant worry and nagging fear. I was so edgy I began snapping at my kids, who were lost in their own pain and bewilderment.

The credit rating we had taken such pride in suffered. We had bought, among other things, a camping trailer that I just couldn't find a buyer for. The payments were three months behind, and the onset of winter threatened to freeze up the pipes before I could get it sold. I began getting up in the middle of cold nights to see if the thermometer had hit lower than 32 degrees.

I closed off the upstairs section of the house and kept the thermostat set at 62 degrees in an effort to reduce heating bills. The three of us huddled together for warmth in the long evenings.

One day I was talking to my grandmother on the phone, complaining about the futility of my situation. "Now, Betty," Gram exclaimed, "where is your faith?"

"Oh, I don't see what even the Lord can do now, Gram," I sighed. "He just isn't giving me any answers. I keep trying to work things out, but—"

"Betty, you keep worrying about everything, and trying to work things out *your* way. Why don't you just have faith and let the Lord do it *His* way? When we hang up, you just go right in and pray for God to take your problems over, then you leave those troubles in His hands and just see what happens."

I promised to do that, and when we'd hung up I went into my bedroom, got down on my knees, and wept, praying, "Lord, I give up. I'm tired, hurt, and beat. If You haven't given up on me, forgive me for my doubt, and strengthen my faith. I know I can't get through this alone, and I'm terrified. Please be with me."

I prayed longer and cried for what seemed like hours. When the words and the tears were finally spent, I collapsed on the bed.

Exactly how I can't say, but slowly a peace came over me, and I rose up from that bed putting all my problems behind me. Later that week, five people wanted to buy the camping trailer. A friend told me about food stamps and partial public assistance. I found I was eligible for both. My husband got a job and started to send support for the kids.

My children perked up and were able to accept that their daddy still loved them but had problems he had to work out. I began waking up every morning so grateful to be alive, so full of faith, so completely aware that we were not alone.

Things are still difficult, especially financially, but now I accept hardship—it gives me an opportunity to express gratitude by keeping this faith. I realize now that the Lord strengthens and teaches us by allowing us to feel heartache. Yes, anyone can believe when life is sunshine, but smiling in life's showers and storms is a miracle of faith!

—B.M., Tennessee

M y car! My baby has been kidnapped!" I screamed after I came out of the sewing center. When I'd gone into the center, Amy, my three-month-old baby, had been sleeping in her car seat. Thinking I'd be just a few minutes in the store to pick up a pattern I had ordered earlier in the week, I'd left her in the backseat of my car. But the clerk was busy and I'd been longer than I'd expected.

A police officer on the corner heard my screams and came over to talk to me, but my car was nowhere in sight.

I called my husband, and he came and took me home. I cried all the way home and sobbed over and over that I was to blame that my baby was gone—that I should have taken her into the store with me. I could just hear my mother saying as she had said so often, "Never leave the baby in the car alone even for one minute!" But it was too late now to think of that.

Neighbors came to console me, but nothing helped. I was too upset. At first I cried and cried; then I just stared into space.

Finally my mother asked, "Where has your faith gone? Remember when Amy was born premature and the doctor didn't think she'd make it? You turned to God and prayed with all your heart many times a day."

I went upstairs to Amy's room and knelt down beside her crib. Tears streaming down my cheeks, I prayed: *Please, God, watch over my baby and bring her back to this crib. Give me a second chance. I'll watch over her day and night.*

For three hours I stayed in her room, praying and praying. Then all at once I felt very calm and in the distance I could hear

Amy crying in the car, which I was certain was parked near the shopping center.

It was evening by then. I got up and went downstairs, went into the kitchen, made the baby's formula, and put it in the refrigerator. Everyone looked at me in amazement.

I told my husband, "Come on—let's look out at the shopping center again."

"But, honey, we have been out there four times already. Besides, the police have a roadblock set up for the kidnapper," he replied.

Mother urged him to go anyway, so we went. We drove through the whole shopping center, but my car was nowhere in sight. I prayed to myself. We drove around the back and down all the roads near the center, but no car.

Then my husband drove down a dead-end road where a small junkyard was. As we neared it, I saw my blue car! "It's my car!" I shouted. My husband hardly stopped his car before I jumped out. My car was all smashed on one side and part of a window was broken, but I could hear my baby crying. That was the sweetest sound I ever heard!

I pulled the door open and picked Amy up. Her booties were kicked off. I hugged her. With tears streaming down my face I knelt down and whispered, "Thank You, God. Thank You!"

We took Amy to the hospital to have her checked. The doctors said she was hungry and a little shook up, but otherwise she was in fine condition. Then my husband called the police. When the officer saw my car, he said, "If I ever saw a miracle, that's one! Having your baby strapped in a well-padded car bed saved her life."

The police figured that when the person who took my car discovered there was a baby in it, he wanted to abandon the car. So he drove fast around the shopping-center corner and hit the steel light pole—there was broken glass on the blacktop and blue paint from my car on the pole.

That's my "miracle of faith." Through prayer, God guided me to my baby. I say a prayer every day for my baby and all the babies in the world, and also for the man who took my car that he will become a better person.

I've told my story over and over to the Mothers' Club where I live, and now I want to tell *all* young mothers never to leave their baby or small children alone in a car. It's very dangerous. I know through experience.

—R.H., Ohio

I had always thought I had a lot of faith in God's willingness and ability to bring me through any sort of trouble—that is, until my husband, Bob, was injured in an automobile accident. He spent three months in a hospital. When the doctors said they had done all they could for him, they sent him home. They told me the broken bones he had sustained had healed, but he was still weak and highly nervous from the shock caused by the impact. The doctors also said his complete recovery would be slow, and the length of time involved would depend largely on the measure of cheerfulness and optimism in our home.

For the first few days after Bob returned home, I was full of hope and high spirits. However, as the days became weeks, each one causing us to dig a little deeper into our small savings account, my spirits drooped lower and lower. Oh, I prayed, but I just didn't have confidence that my prayers were doing any good. I tried hard to conceal my anxiety and depression from Bob and from Patty, our six-year-old daughter, but I realized later that I hadn't fooled either of them.

One morning, Patty unexpectedly came in from playing and found me lying on the couch, my face buried in a sofa pillow to keep Bob from hearing me cry. Patty climbed up beside me, put her arm around me, and patted my shoulder as if she were the mother. "Mommy," she said, "let's say a real hard prayer for Daddy to get well."

"All right, Patty," I said, "let's."

Patty sat up straight on the couch. Out of the corner of my eye, I could see that she had closed her eyes and put her small hands together in innocent supplication. We prayed together for several minutes.

"There!" Patty exclaimed. Her bright face turned up to mine only to see another tear rolling down my cheek.

"Mommy!" she scolded. "You're not supposed to cry anymore. Grandma said that after you pray, you're supposed to be happy. Grandma said that when you ask God to help you, He starts doing it right away!"

It was at that moment that I felt as if a great light had streamed into my darkened consciousness. The example of faith demonstrated by Patty was just what I needed at that moment.

I grabbed Patty in my arms and hugged her tightly. "Of course, darling," I assured her. "Right now, God is helping Daddy to get well."

Patty went happily back outside to play, and I sat thanking God for using my little girl to strengthen my trust in His goodness and mercy.

While reviewing my former feelings, I realized that when Bob had been sent home from the hospital and the doctors had prescribed no medication and had suggested no further visits, I had felt that in spite of my many prayers, nothing was being done to help him. I also realized that Bob had felt and shared my fear and anxiety. *No wonder*, I told myself now, *that he is still despondent, seeing me go around the house with such a long face.*

"God, forgive me," I prayed, "for my lack of faith—for letting my husband down at the very time when he needs me most." Soon I felt that a tremendous weight had been lifted from my heart.

I got up and went into Bob's room. He was lying in bed, staring at the ceiling. The room was dim and depressing. I went over and pulled up the window shades, letting in a burst of sunshine. "My, it's a beautiful day, honey!" I said enthusiastically. "How about going out for a walk?"

Immediately, Bob caught the spirit of my changed feelings. A smile, the first one I'd seen on his face in months, touched his lips. "Okay," he said. "It's about time I got out of this house for a while."

From that day on, I went around the house singing and thinking up cheerful plans to discuss with Bob. If the slightest doubt tried to creep into my mind, I removed it by praying, "Thank You, God, for helping Bob to get well and strong again."

Even though I was expecting good things to happen, I am still surprised at how quickly Bob recovered and went back to work. Every time I look at Patty, I think: *And a little child shall lead them.* She looks at me knowingly when her daddy bounds into the house after work and catches her up in a bear hug. Her expression clearly says: "See? I told you there was nothing to cry about!"

—F.R., Florida

According to the doctor, my aunt was in bad shape. She had fluid surrounding her heart, and her lungs had collapsed, leaving her on a respirator. My family listened as the doctor summed up my aunt's condition. "She has the heart of an eighty-two-year-old." His words shocked me; my aunt was barely sixty-two.

We all had rushed to the hospital when the doctor called and said my aunt might not make it through the night. Knowing that she could die at any time was very hard for me to grasp. I didn't think she was immortal, but she seemed to be in better shape. But now, hours later, she was on her deathbed.

My family began to contemplate on who would make the decision to either keep her on the respirator or take her off. I didn't concentrate on any of that. Instead, I sat at her bedside and took time out to talk to God.

I knew that through prayer, miracles were possible. I knew God could make her well again. I asked God to renew and strengthen her body and spirit, which had been broken before she had taken ill. We held a nightlong vigil for her and prayed God would give her a second chance.

When morning came, my aunt was still in the land of the living. God had given me relief, and I knew I wouldn't have to worry about my aunt's condition any longer. Within a few days, she regained consciousness and three weeks later, she left the hospital.

Although she now needs an oxygen tank to help her breathe, my aunt looks and feels better than she has in years. Before her illness, she couldn't walk more than ten seconds without having to stop and catch her breath. But after her recovery, she is able to walk blocks before she feels tired.

The most wonderful thing was her realization that her recovery was by the grace of God. She knows that she had gone without acknowledging God for a long time. Since then, she has confessed the Lord as her savior and has joined the church. At sixty-four, my aunt is still praising God for her "miracle."

—J.G., Illinois

I realized the meaning of "time stood still" when the surgeon issued the dreaded results of my husband's tests. With blockage in five arteries leading to the heart and one on the left side of his neck leading to the brain, surgery was imminent.

The next day I hurried down the hallway behind my beloved's stretcher on the way to the operating room. The nurse paused at the door and said, "Tell him good-bye." Good-bye had a new meaning. I leaned over, kissed him, and said, "Have a good sleep." Fighting back tears, I hurried toward the double doors of the waiting room to our sons, their wives, and my parents. The long vigil began. Silently I prayed that our thirty-four years together were not over. Married young, our love still remained strong.

After several hours in surgery, we were allowed into the intensive care unit to see our loved one. His tall frame lay helplessly connected to tubes and monitors. I held his hand as he drifted in slumber.

Anxiously, I waited for the eight-thirty visitation. The waiting room overflowed with friends and family members gathered to see patients. A foreboding enveloped me. Even though we were told, "They're just behind and need to do a little cleaning up," I knew something was wrong.

Finally, the surgeon came to us and said, "We're taking him back to surgery. He's losing blood much too fast. We can't find out why."

By eleven-thirty P.M., I was trembling and prayed, "Please, Lord, grant us more time together." At twelve-thirty, the tired surgeon announced, "He'll be okay. The blood loss is slowing. We had to open him back up and find out why."

The next morning, I knelt in the hospital chapel and gave thanks for God's mercy. The following day Mother and I stood on either side of my husband's bed. He asked through the oxygen mask if he was in surgery long. I casually answered, "Oh, quite a while." Vividly I remembered the twelve traumatic hours of waiting.

He looked up and said, "I went two times and an angel went with me both times." He raised one hand and crooked his fingers in a walking motion through the air. "She walked along beside me in a bright light."

Mother and I exchanged startled glances. He had never regained consciousness between the two trips to surgery. No one had mentioned the second time to him. My eyes misted as I gripped his hand tightly, unable to speak. After a silence, Mother tenderly touched his arm and said, "Yes, I'm sure an angel did go with you." I believe with all my heart that God did answer my prayers and led him through the valley of darkness.

—J.I.K., Missouri

It was a wet and humid morning as I drove my husband to work. He worked on top of a mountain at an Army retreat center. I was driving a rental car since our car was being repaired. As I was driving and half listening to my one-year-old daughter, I thought about the grocery list that I had made. I was not in the mood to go to the commissary, however, my brother was with us for a visit and he wanted to see the facilities.

When we finally reached the retreat center our rental car was smoking. My husband went inside to get water for the radiator. Meanwhile, I was trying to tell him that driving that car was dangerous. He said not to worry, so I started the car. Our daughter wanted to sit in the front with her uncle, so he strapped her in.

As I drove down the steep mountain road, I thought about what I would fix for supper that night. Rounding the corner, I pressed the brakes and nothing happened. I pressed and pumped the brakes, meanwhile yelling to my brother that the brakes weren't working. The road was curvy and I was having trouble staying on the road. At that moment, I realized how beautiful life was and how much I wanted to live. My brother yelled to pull the emergency brake, but I couldn't seem to do it while keeping my eyes on the road.

Just when I thought there was no hope in sight, I felt this strange power take over for me and turn the steering wheel. As our car went off the road, I screamed. In a couple of moments, the car stopped after bumping into a tree.

My brother gave a sigh of relief and asked, "Are you hurt?" My daughter, who thought we just went for a joy ride, was no worse for wear.

When we got out of the smoking car, I realized just how lucky we really were. God, I know in my heart, had managed to drive the car very neatly between two cement posts, down an incline, and smack center into a tree. He saved our lives.

Still in shock, we started walking up the mountain road. My brother said that he would run up the rest of the way, and let my husband know what had happened.

Later, when talking to the M.P.s, they confided that I must have been an excellent driver to stop the car as I did. I just smiled and whispered, "Thank you, God."

—R.F., Hawaii

I can still remember the days before Hurricane Andrew struck some parts of Louisiana. My family and I were shocked by its determination to travel the distance. This powerful force had already rocked Florida, and now it was headed our way. I realized that the Lord was going to be called upon by many, so I made communication with Him right away.

While everyone wished the hurricane would take another path, I only prayed that it would spare many lives. I had faith that the Lord would find a way.

The day before the hurricane struck, we finally realized that Andrew was determined to speak his mind. Many families, as well as my own, tied things down and packed up to go to our hurricane shelter. I spoke to the Lord once again and asked for His help. I knew He'd be there since He'd always been there before when I needed His help. He always gave me the strength to go on in hard times. I prayed that we might still have a place to live, but most of all I prayed that everyone would survive.

Early on the morning the hurricane struck, I sat quietly. I still had faith that the Lord would see us through. The winds were truly strong as they banged against our shelter. Although I was a bit shaken by the force of the storm, I knew I had something stronger—faith in the Lord.

We witnessed all sorts of destruction from the storm—fallen trees and power lines—on our way home from the shelter. When we reached our home, I finally realized that, once again, the Lord had answered our prayers. Not only did we have our lives, but we also had our home. Others, unfortunately, were not as lucky when it came to their homes, but they had the gift of life.

It's been a while since the storm, but some of its effects are still here. Many people have attempted to rebuild their homes and are trying to go on with their lives. We have all been helped by kind strangers and wish to thank them all. If it weren't for their donations and time, many would not have made it.

The Lord's faith gave many people heart—the heart to help their brothers and sisters. All of the Lord's children came together and realized that without one another, they couldn't survive. For those who doubt, the Lord will always work it out. If one has faith, He will never let you down.

—V.W., Louisiana

I became born-again late in my life. When in my teens, I had studied and was saved by a kind neighbor. But I began to realize that deep down I did not have the faith that would sustain me through good times and bad.

Thirty years later, I had gone through a marriage, two children, and divorce, still refusing to accept that faith could move mountains. I raised my children alone and then remarried. We had a daughter and I found out I was pregnant. The doctor told me I had a problem that might progress to cancer. My husband moved out and my life became a hell on earth. When I had exhausted all I thought would bring him back, I wound up on my knees—I knew this was my last hope. I did not know how to pray, so I began a dialogue with God, telling Him things I had told no one. I promised Him that if He would hold me together, I would learn to have faith. He did.

My crisis of faith came barely seven months later. I had delivered a son, had surgery for cancer, and my husband returned home. I thought that it would be smooth sailing. My oldest son had gone white-water rafting with a group of friends. That afternoon, I was in the kitchen when I suddenly knew in the pit of my stomach that something had happened to my son. It was an overwhelming feeling that he was in deep trouble. I called my husband and he told me to calm down. I tried to, but the feeling would not go away. Finally, I went to my room and knelt. I asked Jesus to tell me if my son was hurt, dying, or safe. I began to feel very warm and the feeling in my chest and stomach began to lessen. I had the sensation of being cradled. I told my husband that something had happened to our son, but he was okay now.

It was almost two and a half hours later that we got the call from our son to meet him at the hospital. He had been caught up against the side of a rock, stood to dislodge, and his partner accidentally dropped his oar into the water. When the canoe shot backward, my son was thrown out into the rapids. Since the rocks were dense, he was saved from being swept down the river. Everyone formed a human chain to get him out of the water, but the current was too strong. He would try to swim for shore and was constantly thrown back into the rocks. Finally, after an hour of attempts, he was able to swim out of the current. At the hospital, they found no fractures, just a lot of contusions and scrapes.

My son told me later that he was so tired and weak from fighting the current and the rocks, but suddenly he felt a renewal of strength and when he struck out that last time, he knew that he would make it. I know in my heart that he had a hand that was stretching from above, to me and to him. At last I could say for certain that if you have faith that you exercise, there is nothing impossible.

—C.K.S., New York

My son, Ron, had planned to be a Navy chaplain, but he died of cancer during his senior year of high school. It was easy for me to turn part of my wrath toward God. He had the power to save my son. God could have placed the idea of taking a biopsy in the mind of one of the many doctors who had said there was nothing seriously wrong with Ron.

After Ron's death, it took many weeks of prayer to put me on speaking terms with God, and I gradually learned that He never shuts one door in a person's life without opening others.

I was seeking something to help me find an outlet for my hurt and grief. A door to the writing field was opened when I finished some of Ron's manuscripts. A friend had asked, "Have you ever thought of writing inspirational stories?"

"Not me," I'd said. "I don't even like to write letters." But that attitude soon changed.

A conflict in our family was tearing me apart, and it seemed writing about it was the only therapy I could find. When I shared the story with a friend who was having similar trouble, she urged me to send my story to a magazine. Much to my surprise, my story was published.

The same day that I received payment for the story, a letter came, asking our family to sponsor an American Indian boy. We saw this commitment as a living memorial to Ron. What better way to remember our beloved son than to provide for a less fortunate boy?

Letters from Ed, our foster son—thanking us for new shoes and clothing—seemed to arrive at times when I was most depressed. Cards on special days, especially Mother's Day, would bring tears as I remembered my freckle-faced boy who would give me funny handmade cards that said "I love you, Mom."

Late in 1974, the years of suppressed anger and grief took their toll. I suffered a nervous breakdown, and shut myself off from everyone except my husband. He begged me to get help, but I refused. I didn't want to face the stigma I thought was attached to people who went to "shrinks." The cost of long-term therapy could be expensive, too, and it would mean the end of sponsoring Ed, who was then thirteen. Most people wanted younger children, and the agency might not find another sponsor to replace us. Besides, how would Ed feel if we stopped helping him? He would probably have to quit school. He was already several grades behind. It could destroy his faith in humanity.

The anniversary of Ron's birthday was a bleak, snowy day, like the day Ron died. My husband hesitated about leaving me alone that morning. "I wish everyone would get off my back!" I screamed.

For several hours I sat holding my Bible and crying. *Oh, God.* I finally prayed, *Jesus promised. "I will not leave you comfortless. I will come to you." Where is He?*

Then a voice within me said: *I'm here, but you don't listen. The only way you become separated from God is in your thinking.*

I don't know how long it took me to decide on calling the Mental Health Association, but soon I found my trembling fingers had dialed the number. "If a person needed help with depression, where would he go?" I asked.

"If he's a veteran, we suggest the Veterans Hospital. If not, get him to come here," a woman told me.

"Thank you," I said, hanging up before she could ask any questions.

I think I said "he" because I didn't want the stranger on the other end of the line to know that I was the one who needed help. Or had Something Else made me use the word "he"? (When I checked several months later, the girl said she wouldn't have suggested the Veterans Hospital for a woman. She was not aware that there are so many women veterans.)

Because I'd been in the Service, I was entitled to be treated as an outpatient at the Veterans Hospital. I received therapy for the next eighteen months. With the burden of expensive medical care gone, we were able to keep providing the needs of our foster son. The Lord does work in many ways.

I believe that God, in His own unusual way, is using me and my husband to help repay a debt long overdue our American Indian brothers. And once again, during the long, sometimes painful sessions of therapy, He opened new doors for me, making me more aware of the divine potential in myself and others.

The understanding of my family, the hospital staff, and the other patients gave me the courage to walk across the bridge of spiritual awakening that God offers to everyone who asks. My writing has been published by seven denominations, and I am grateful for the joy of reaching out to others who hurt.

I'm not saying the "blah" days don't return occasionally. But now, when I feel stress and depression closing in—as everyone does at times—I find a quiet spot and listen for the voice of God within me saying: *I am here. I care.*

—M.B., Missouri

It was an unusually hot muggy day late in April, and already the sun was beating down mercilessly. *Bet I'll be able to fry an egg on the sidewalk by noon*, I thought dismally.

How I hated these hot, humid days! I spent them mounted on a tractor seat beneath an unrelenting sun, eating what seemed like bushels of sand and dirt from the dry fields.

Jeanie and the children had finished their breakfast and were starting out for school. I had been the school bus driver for several years; but when field work lagged behind, Jeanie drove for me.

The ground needed moisture badly. It had been an unusually

dry month, but today there were scattered rain clouds all around us and predictions were for a downpour by tonight.

"Don't plan to see me until late this afternoon, Rob," Jeanie reminded me. "I've lots of shopping to do, and Pastor Marks and Judy and I plan to drive over to Joliet for the new junior choir robes today."

It was later in the afternoon and skies were indeed beginning to cloud up. I had decided to push on in the hopes that I could finish this field before I got soaked.

Suddenly, for no apparent reason, I stopped halfway across a row. It was 2:15 in the afternoon. In less than thirty minutes Jeanie would be starting home with a bus load of youngsters. Why did that thought suddenly send a chill through me? It never had before, and she had been substitute driver for me all spring. As I pondered this thought, another chill shook me, and an apprehensive fear clutched at me, obliterating all thoughts of my unfinished field. I searched the sky and saw nothing the least bit threatening, yet my ominous feeling persisted.

"Lord," I shouted, "is this Your way of showing me that something is wrong? Is Jeanie headed for an accident? Please, Lord, if something is wrong, give me a sign—a loud crack of thunder, a bolt of lightning. Something!"

Still no sign. No thunder, no lightning, not even a darkened sky, and yet my foreboding depression remained. I wondered why I had this feeling, and then realization struck.

That must be it! I thought. *This feeling I have must be the sign I asked for. Jeanie must be in danger. I'm almost sure there's an accident about to happen.*

Never had I driven back across the fields so fast. I didn't even stop to open the pasture gate. I just drove over it in my frantic haste. I didn't stop to climb out of my dusty field clothes either, but just jumped into the pickup and sped to town. Within minutes my wife would be leaving the schoolyard and, I felt certain, would be driving into some unknown danger.

I pulled into the schoolyard just as Jeanie was closing the bus door. She had forty-three youngsters aboard.

"For goodness sakes, Rob," she cried when she saw me, "what are you doing here dressed like that?"

"There isn't time to explain," I answered. "Just take Danny and Mary Ann home with you in the pickup, and I'll drive the bus tonight."

The rest of what happened that day made newspaper headlines. It all happened so fast, though, that there was little time to think.

I had driven several miles and safely delivered some of the children when the sky suddenly darkened and it became frighteningly still. I hurried along as fast as I dared, trying to drop off as many of the youngsters as possible before the rains came, double-checking each intersection, still fearing the disaster of my premonition. Suddenly, looming straight ahead of me, came the unmistakable funnel cloud of a tornado. It was low, seemingly touching the ground, and I could see no possible avenue of escape for us. I slammed the bus to a halt and threw open the door.

I shouted, "Children, hurry! Jump out and lie flat, face down in the ditch. That tornado is going to hit us!"

I knew now why God had sent me in Jeanie's place this afternoon. She would surely have been too terrified to take command of the situation.

Children react so quickly to a sudden command in a crisis that within seconds the bus was emptied and all of the children were facedown in the ditch with me. Seconds later the tornado struck, crushing our bus like a broken match stick and sending metal debris raining down on us. When it was over, what was left of the bus lay strewn over the road and adjacent fields. No one could possibly have survived in it.

Help was summoned and the frightened youngsters were taken to the hospital to be examined. Many had cuts and bruises from flying rocks and metal debris, and one little girl had a broken arm, but all were alive because I had heard God's word, and obeyed.

For my family and the families of the other children on that ill-fated school bus, it was most certainly a miracle of faith.

—Anonymous

Being superintendent of a junior Sunday school department is a demanding responsibility, but one which I have found to be very rewarding. Several years ago, though, with the beginning of the church year fast approaching, I found myself without a teacher for the nine-year-old boys. All the men whom I approached had a good reason for not accepting the job. Some were already committed for other classes; others had to work occasionally on Sunday; still others just felt they were not suitable.

Jimmy H. was a good prospect, since he had taught for several years and had an excellent rapport with the pupils. "Would you consider it at all?" I asked him desperately several times, and each time his answer was no. He advanced numerous reasons why he did not feel he could take the class.

As the days passed, I telephoned more and more church members, asking them to help me find a teacher for my boys. All my friends were harassed constantly by my pleadings, but still no positive results.

There was just one Sunday remaining before the new year started. "Who else can I ask?" By this time, I was talking to myself in an effort to solve my dilemma. Suddenly, like a bright flash, the answer came to me. *Ask God!* I fell on my knees and prayed earnestly, "Dear God, please send me a Sunday school teacher. I'm leaving it in Your hands."

With an easy mind, I then headed toward the church. As I walked across the grass, I heard someone shouting at me: "Say, Mrs. Lewis, do you still need a Sunday school teacher? If you do, here I am!" Jimmy H. stood there grinning.

"Gosh, I sure *do* need you. When did you change your mind?" I asked.

"While I was shaving this morning, I just looked at myself in the mirror and suddenly all my excuses melted away. I felt I *had* to take that class," he answered.

Upon further discussion, we found that he had made his decision at the exact time I was on my knees talking to God!

—E.G.L., Florida

I used to complain about my perceived misfortunes until I met a man who taught me that truly lucky people are those who realize how blessed they are and make the most of each day.

When I met my future husband, I thought he was the most eligible bachelor in the world. We met in a hardware store, of all places. He was every girl's fantasy. We got to talking about every-thing from three-penny nails to pizza. Turns out we liked a lot of the same things and we just seemed to click. Something about his warm and open attitude seemed to temper my usual brisk cyni-cism. He wasn't at all like the men I usually met. Not only was he good-looking, but so kind and thoughtful, with a sense of humor and sunny disposition.

As I was leaving the store, he asked me out. I couldn't believe it. What a dream come true! I felt like a contestant on reality TV that wins the date with the hunk! This is too good to be real, the cynical part of me echoed in the back of my mind, but something about his smile made me want to believe in fairy tales.

Our romance blossomed and we began to see each other al-most every day. One Saturday, he came over right after getting a haircut. When he turned around, I noticed two very large, well-defined scalp scars that hadn't been noticeable before. I hesitated asking him about them. Perhaps someday he'll tell me about this past injury, I thought to myself.

I was so blinded by love I didn't notice his little quirks—how sometimes he'd bump into me when we were walking together, how he sometimes faded off into a sort of dream while wide awake. He did carpentry work, but chose simple tools over power tools that would do the job much faster. I'm ashamed to admit, I was too caught up in how much attention he was pouring on me to notice some really important things about him.

One night, we just began talking about our future, which was definitely leaning toward marriage. He said we needed to have a se-rious talk; that he had to tell me about his past so that I could make an informed decision about spending the rest of my life with him. My mind considered a million possibilities. Could it be an ex-wife? Kids? Or was he keeping a secret about a felony conviction in his past? As if we both recognized the shift in atmosphere—from romantic dreaming to stark reality—we got up from the floor where we were cuddling and sat down at my kitchen table. I sat across from him, staring intently into those green eyes. I clutched my coffee cup, braced to face whatever he felt he needed to confess.

"I had a brain tumor," he blurted out. "It was five years ago. Very large, not cancerous, thank God. However, they had to operate or I would've died. The operation was successful in that I got to live and have most of my sight, but I do have some severe vision field cut in my left eye and sometimes suffer petit mal seizures. Those times you might've thought that I wasn't paying attention, I was just not able to pay attention, at least temporarily until the seizure passed. I try to do my best each day to work with my disability. Sometimes I still get severe headaches; the doctors say that's normal and stress seems to trigger the seizures. And I do apologize if I sometimes bump into you. I was so embarrassed at what you might've thought!" He chuckled with that last comment, then leaned in and held my hands in his. "I have what people would call good days and bad days. I choose to call most days good days because I'm alive and am doing much better than many brain tumor survivors. If you still want to stay with me, after knowing this, I would like to bring you to a support group I attend for people with traumatic brain injuries and brain tumor survivors, and their spouses. Would you be interested?" he asked with an expression that melted my heart.

I stared into my coffee cup for a moment, and then looked up into those gorgeous green eyes. I took a deep breath and then replied that I'd be very interested in being his wife, in learning all I could about his challenges, and that I'd be proud to live my life with such a brave, positive person. I jumped across the table and into the arms of my Survivor Hunk, a pet name I have for my man, who is a walking miracle.

We've just celebrated our sixth anniversary and my husband's courage and cheerful outlook on life reminds me what a fortunate girl I am, after all.

—V.F., Texas

C ancer. The word I'd never wanted to hear froze my senses for a moment. A few years ago I'd been to see my doctor, and he'd requested that I come back a few days later so he could discuss my pathology report with me.

"Would you mind going over it again?" I asked. "I'm not sure I understand."

He explained that I had Atypical Adenomatous Hyperplasia, or in simpler words, precancerous cells in my uterus. A few cases would respond to medical treatment without removing the uterus. But this was more likely to happen if the condition was caught early. In my case, he recommended surgery. He only agreed to put off the surgery for three months and see if prescription drugs would work after I pleaded with him.

My husband and I had barely been married two years. I couldn't let this happen. We wanted to have children. I don't remember leaving the doctor's office. I was in a daze because my doctor hadn't given me much hope.

Tears rolled down my face as I drove home and tried to keep my eyes on the road. How could I tell my husband? Finally I decided there was no best way, just the simple truth.

My husband met me at the door and immediately saw the

grief-stricken terror in my eyes. I told him what had happened at the doctor's office. Afterwards, he held me in his arms and assured me that we'd work it out together.

That evening we hurried to a bookstore and bought everything we could find about hyperplasia. I stayed up half the night reading and studying every line, wishing that somewhere it would describe my symptoms as being in the early stage. But I didn't find it.

After I had taken all of the pills the doctor prescribed and more tests were run, the doctor announced that the results had come back positive. The cancerous cells were still there.

I couldn't believe it. I had been feeling better.

His nurse handed me the necessary papers I'd need for admission and I went to the hospital to have my blood work done. While I was there a nurse asked me if I had any questions about my surgery. I did. I had plenty. She said she could see that I wasn't ready for the operation, suggesting that I go back and talk with my doctor again. Or maybe I'd feel better about it if I got a second opinion.

I knew my doctor's thoughts. He treated me as long as he could without taking a risk. This was a Friday and my surgery was scheduled for the following Tuesday.

I went home and told my husband what the nurse had said. In my heart, I couldn't give up. I'd prayed about it and something kept telling me I'd improved.

The following Monday, I canceled my surgery. By Wednesday I had an appointment with another gynecologist who'd been highly recommended by a friend. This time the doctor was a woman. After looking at my records, she agreed to treat me for an additional three months, making it clear to me that my condition had to be reckoned with, one way or the other, at that time.

"Please, dear God, help me," I prayed. "I don't want to have cancer." I believed in my heart that He would help me.

My spirit was filled with hope as I waited for the results of my final tests. When I saw the doctor, she said there wasn't a trace of the cancer cells. They were gone.

Every day I thank the good Lord for placing the right people in my path when I needed them—the nurse at the hospital, the doctor who gave me a second chance, and my loving husband who stood beside me and never gave up hope. His love was there when I needed it most. I have a new lease on life.

—A.B., Oklahoma

When my husband had to have an emergency triple bypass, he gave me his watch and ring for safekeeping. He had the ring for forty years and it meant a lot to him.

After he spent four days in intensive care, I discovered his ring was missing. I'd been living out of the trunk of the car, not daring to leave the hospital, and sleeping in the waiting room until he was assigned a room. I looked through all the things I'd used and searched the waiting room area. Security was called and all stations were notified of the missing ring. I searched the car, but had no luck. I didn't dare tell my dear husband I'd lost his ring. My precious, ever-present daughter told me that I would find it, and my dear friend said, "Nothing is lost in the sight of God. You will find it."

After two weeks, my husband was released from the hospital. I took out an ad in the newspaper, hoping someone had found the missing ring. Finally, my husband asked for his watch, which I gave him, and then his ring. I started to cry and told him that I'd lost his cherished ring. He was very quiet, which made me feel worse. My prayer was always that God would help me find the ring.

During the months that followed, we talked about getting a new car, but I was attached to my car and I loved keeping it like new inside and out. Exactly nine months after my husband's surgery and days before his seventy-third birthday I was once again cleaning the trunk of my car when I spotted what looked like a key chain. I flicked it up from a very small crevice way down in the trunk and, miracle of miracles, I found the ring! I cried and thanked God.

When I approached my husband with my hands behind my back, I said, "Which hand?" He was astounded and so thankful that his ring had been found. I said, "Happy birthday, honey."

—D.B., Texas

In 1994, I went into the hospital for a hysterectomy. I had cervical cancer and was praying for a miracle. At forty-five, I was expecting my first grandchild in early spring.

I was determined not to undergo chemotherapy or radiation treatments. I had faith that prayer would pull me through. God would cure me. The congregation of my church was lifting me up through prayer.

When I awoke after the surgery, I was in agony. All through

the night, pain ripped through my body. I couldn't hold anything in my stomach. I was freezing. No amount of painkillers helped, nor did the mountains of blankets that the nurses heaped on my bed.

At this point, I placed myself in God's hands. "Thy will be done, Father," I whispered.

Some time during the night, a nurse I'd never seen before entered my room. I couldn't tear my eyes from her face. She looked so serene. Through a haze of pain, I noticed that her skin was perfectly smooth and shiny. She was the most beautiful person I had ever seen.

She placed her hand on my forehead and pushed my hair back from my face. Immediately, warmth enveloped my entire body.

"You'll be just fine," she soothed. "That grandson of yours will soon be sleeping in your arms."

"How do you know?" I rasped.

"There are some things I just know," she answered. She tucked the blankets firmly around me and turned to leave.

"What's your name?" I murmured.

"Trudy," she replied, and then she was gone.

The next morning, I inquired at the nurses station about Trudy. No one knew who Trudy was, but my day nurse offered to check with personnel. The result? There was no one named Trudy at the hospital.

Almost five years later, I am cancer-free and taking care of my grandsons. Yes, I have two.

I believe that when I put myself in God's hands He cured me. As for Trudy, I believe she was a special messenger sent by God to reassure and comfort me in my time of need.

—M.M.A., Canada

One summer day, twenty-four years ago, I was playing out in the yard with my children and to my surprise, my mother pulled up in front of the house. I knew something was wrong because she never visited me during the week. She got out of the car, and I could see she had been crying. I asked what was wrong, and she told me she had just left the doctor's office with my brother: he had been diagnosed with leukemia.

I couldn't believe that my only brother, who was only twelve years old, had been diagnosed with such a frightening disease. What made it worse was that the doctor only gave my brother six months to live. I thought I was in a dream.

My brother endured months of pain. It was very stressful to all of us at the time. The days were so long, and we were at our wits' end. Then our doctor told us about an experimental drug being tested on patients suffering from leukemia. We all hesitated at first, but our love for my brother was too powerful. We would've tried anything to make him better. I loved my brother, and I wasn't going to stand by and let him die.

Nothing happened at first. His condition remained the same until one day, my brother got out of bed, walked out into the hospital hallway, and asked a nurse for a hamburger. We instantly knew that he was going to be fine. We knew that God had healed him.

And thirty-six years later, my brother is living his life to the fullest.

—C.M., North Carolina

It was a mild winter day. I'd just turned four years old and my neighbor, my brother, and I were playing on the frozen creek behind our house. Our parents were struggling to make ends meet, so instead of having skates we used old rubber boots we'd gotten as hand-me-downs.

It started out as a fun day. We'd run and slide on the ice, fall down, and get up and do it all over again. Then I noticed a wet spot on the ice where the creek started to bend. I remember telling the other two boys to stay clear of the wet spot because they might fall in.

As time went on, the wet spot had gotten bigger. The loose snow had camouflaged it so it wasn't that noticeable. I guess I had slid a little too hard or too fast when I fell in and went deep into the cold creek. The current carried me swiftly downstream. I could hear my neighbor and my brother screaming for help.

Now, I want you to know I didn't know too much about the Lord at that time. But I did say my prayers before going to bed at night. As I continued to drift downstream I heard a voice say, "Don't panic. Whatever you do, don't panic. I'm with you." As I got to the bend in the creek the voice told me to reach up and grab the icicles hanging down from the layers of ice covering the creek. And I did just that. But my head was submerged under the water and I wondered how I'd breathe. Again the voice told me not to panic. It said I should pull myself up between the spaces of water and ice and breathe the air in those pockets. It worked!

I could hear my brother and my neighbor yelling my name. I yelled to them that I was okay. None of us knew what to do next. Then the voice explained that I should head back to the spot where I fell into the water, grabbing on to the icicles to help move me in that direction. I did just as the voice told me and soon my brother and neighbor were helping me out of the water.

As we walked back to the house so that I could get dry and warm, I looked back at the hole in the ice and said to my brother, "I'll remember this day and what happened for the rest of my life. And I'll remember the voice of the angel that saved me." Of course, my brother looked at me like I was crazy.

I'm almost fifty now, and my brother is a preacher. To this day we both remember that winter day. I thank God for saving my life, and for allowing me to experience every day since that accident.

—D.M., Michigan

As the mother of two children, my mornings were hectic. The day was full of housework and errands to run. Dinnertime came quickly. After clearing the table, I was ready for time to myself, which meant going to bingo. We would take turns driving between friends. My neighbor said she'd drive. After placing my supplies and purse in her car, I removed my wedding band, placed it on top of her car, and applied some lotion to my dry hands. I stepped in the car and off we went. The trip was a short one—just around the corner.

Settling down at the bingo hall with my boards, I rubbed my hands and realized that my ring wasn't on. Needless to say, I was numb with shock.

Returning to my home that evening only meant one thing—searching in the dark for a small piece of gold that had many memories wrapped around every scratch and dent.

Three women scavenging in the dark with flashlights quickly brought the attention of the local police. After hearing my story, they joined in the search. We quit about an hour and a half later. Crying, I went to bed. On my left hand was an indentation of my wedding band that I'd worn for sixteen years. My heart ached.

I decided I needed help. I opened my heart and soul to Jesus in prayer. I am not a religious person, but I asked Jesus to help me. I figured that if it was meant to be, I would need strength to accept the fact that my ring was lost forever. I also asked in a humble way for the Lord to help me find my ring.

The next morning, I was up at the crack of dawn. I searched the area again so long that my neck hurt. I called the street department and asked them not to sweep that day and explained my ordeal.

My desire to find my ring was all-consuming. I could not function during normal everyday activities. When my neighbor returned that day, I asked in desperation if we could reenact the events of the previous night. Soon my husband's ring had a sturdy piece of dental floss tied to it. I placed his ring on top of the car where I had put mine the night before, and we drove the same route. When we turned the corner, his ring flew off the top of the car. Now I had the general idea where my ring would have landed. We parked the car and started to search again the area that we checked the night before.

Well, you wouldn't believe what happened next. I spotted my ring laying there on the road just waiting to be found. I couldn't believe it! Like my neighbor said, "Your husband's ring was looking for its mate."

I'm grateful that I have my ring. I'm also happy that the Lord heard my prayer and helped me. My mother always told me that if you're helpless and can no longer control a situation, put your cares in the hands of Jesus. Only He knows our fate. He sure knew mine.

—K.B., New Jersey

My miracle of faith took twenty-five years to happen, but it was worth the wait. Our parents divorced after a rocky marriage that produced four children in eight years. I'm the oldest. I remember us kids going back and forth between our mother and father because of court-ordered visitation. Our parents hated each other. We were emotional casualties in their war.

We grew up and made our own lives. Our parents could barely keep a civil tongue whenever they saw each other. When I married my husband neither of them could be in my wedding party. I had to seat them at opposite ends of the ballroom. I considered myself lucky that they both attended.

I tried hard to make my wedding special. I wanted it to be a spiritual experience for everyone that attended. We prayed that our wedding would be peaceful and that God would be with us. Silently, I asked for my parents' hearts to be more open, and that they could be friendly with one another. I knew it would take a miracle, so I asked for one. I felt I was crazy to expect anything like that, but I hoped it would happen.

When we came back from our honeymoon, my sister called us, all excited. She told me that after my husband and I left the reception hall, she saw our parents having a drink together. When she and her boyfriend finally left the hall, our parents were still there talking!

I called my dad right away. It was true. Our parents had approached each other at my reception and ended up toasting to my happiness! While we were on our honeymoon, they even had dinner together.

Nothing made me happier than seeing our parents set aside their differences and talk and visit one another. Except six months later—when they announced their plans to remarry! We're still all in shock. It's wonderful to watch the two of them together. They're like two different people these days. It's a lifelong dream come true. God really performed a miracle.

—D.D.T., New York

My husband had just received a transfer to another state for his job. He had gone ahead to check on our new house while my daughter, my two sons, and I stayed behind to wait for the movers and to pack our belongings.

My older son, who was six at this time, was a friendly fellow. He had long, dark eyelashes and dark brown eyes—everyone noticed them right away. He was always in a happy mood and if you were sad, he never failed to make you laugh.

One night, my oldest son was keeping me company while I

fixed supper for the family. We talked and laughed together while waiting for my husband to call about our new home. It was a happy night.

I decided to pack a few things while I was waiting. My son lay near me, on the floor, watching me pack and talking to me. While my back was turned, my younger son, who was four, went into the closet and took out a gun my husband had for protection. The gun accidentally went off and hit my oldest son.

As fast as I could, I rushed him to the hospital in the car. But there just wasn't enough time. He died, in my arms, on the way to the hospital.

My husband flew down to be with us that night and we all stayed at my brother-in-law's. The children were out playing in the backyard while my husband sat on the front porch. He asked God to just give him one sign that our son was safe with him in heaven. I came outside to see how he was and to check on the children.

All of a sudden, the children started to scream. I looked up, ran into the house, and called everyone outside. Up in the sky was a bright light that grew closer and closer. When it got so close we could almost reach up and touch it, the light curved upward and ascended into the heavens.

The next day, we checked our findings with the local airport, police, and Air Force to see if anyone else had reported this phenomenon, but no one had. My family was the only witness to this incredible occurrence.

We knew, then, that this was the sign from God my husband had prayed for earlier. Because of our prayers and our faith in God, we were given the assurance that our son was safe and sound with our Lord in heaven.

—L.B., Michigan

I have never been a religious person. In fact, there have been times I have doubted whether God exists at all. That changed for me one evening when I needed Him more than I ever had, and He answered my prayers.

My husband, Ray, and I had wanted children from the day we were married. Finally, after being married for five years, we decided to have a baby. I got pregnant right away, and nine months later we had twins, Karen and Michelle. They were both fussy babies, but I didn't mind, at first. I was tired most of the time, but I thought it was the price I had to pay for being so lucky.

After about four months I began to really resent all the time and attention the twins needed. Then I felt guilty for thinking this way. After all, these were two helpless babies I really loved. Ray realized how miserable I was becoming, and he thought I was just tired from taking care of the twins day and night. He helped out with the housework and cooking, but I would snap at him and criticize whatever he did to help. We began to argue frequently.

Finally one night my patience just snapped. Ray came home from work complaining about what a miserable day he'd had and I started screaming at him. I ran out of the house, leaving Ray to cope with the twins. I don't know what I intended to do, but all I really wanted was to throw myself under a bus.

I walked for hours, trying to figure out how the life I had wanted so much had become such a burden to me. Then I saw that I was in front of a church—one I had driven by hundreds of times without giving a second glance. I was drawn inside and I knelt down. Without realizing it I began to pray. Thoughts came into my mind. I remembered my mother, and how much she had loved me and my two sisters. Then I remembered the times that she had lost her patience with us. It seemed that her love overshadowed her anger by far.

Slowly it came to me that it might be natural to want time for myself. Maybe I wasn't the only person in the world who felt this way. I left the church a long time later, feeling renewed and hopeful. God had given me the wisdom I needed to handle my feelings. I went home, suddenly missing my babies.

Since that night, my life has improved dramatically. I get together with other young mothers once a week to talk. We all have a lot of the same problems and feelings, and it helps us to realize that we aren't alone. Whenever I begin to feel overwhelmed, when I lose my patience and am at the end of my rope, I take a few minutes to pray. I ask God for strength, and I always feel better. I thank God for His help. My life has been so much better since I found Him.

—D.P., New York

One fateful morning was the beginning of a nightmare for my family and me. A few days before that, my husband had been to the doctor and given a diagnosis of strep throat. He was given an antibiotic and sent on his way. But instead of getting better, he got worse.

Luckily we got him to the hospital in time to save his life. He went into a condition where all body functions but the heart try to shut down. They put him on a life-support system and put him in their intensive-care unit. For three days, they tried to get his condition stabilized, and finally transferred him to another hospital, one of the best in the country.

At that hospital, he was put in the intensive-care unit, where he hovered between life and death. Things were like a blur for me. The doctors explained to me that my husband's condition was very grave. They said that his kidneys had shut down and that his high fever was making him fight for every breath.

After talking to the doctors and spending a while with my husband, I was going home for some rest. My faith was at an all-time low! How could God leave me alone, when my husband was my strength, my love, and my partner for life? How could I raise five children by myself?

When I got off the elevator to head home, a voice seemed to call me from the hospital chapel. I took a seat in the deserted chapel and began to pray. "Lord, please let him live! Your will be done. I know You will heal him. Please give me a sign that he will be okay!"

Instantly a warmth spread over me, and I felt entirely at peace. I knew that my husband's life was in God's hands, but I also knew He was there with me.

As I reached the parking lot and neared our car, something on the ground glistened, and I looked down. At my feet was the figure of Jesus, lost from someone's crucifix. I picked it up, all the while knowing that it was the sign that I had asked for.

I returned to the hospital early the next morning, dreading what would happen, yet knowing that everything would be all right. The doctors approached me as soon as I walked into the intensive-care ward.

"Your husband has passed the crisis. He will be fine! His fever broke last night about ten o'clock, and his kidneys have begun to function on their own again. We will be able to discontinue the dialysis at once," the doctor said.

Today my husband is fine, except that he has to take an oral medication for diabetes. The doctors can find no medical explanations for the fact that he's alive. Clinically, for a time, he was considered beyond hope. The doctors call him a walking, talking miracle. So do I. Every day I thank God for all the blessings He has bestowed on this family.

—D.A., Michigan

In my hometown, when you turn eighteen, you go to work in the factory. It's expected—everyone does it. But when *I* turned eighteen, I left for bigger and better places. I ended up in Texas, over 1,000 miles away.

Even though I found a job as a cashier and worked hard, I never seemed to have enough money. I couldn't find an apartment I could afford, and the motel I was staying at was taking almost all I earned. I had to wash my clothes in the sink, and one week all I had to eat was a box of crackers and water. I prayed every night, hoping that God would hear and help me out of this horrible situation.

Then my hours at work got cut. I scrimped as much as possible, but I soon fell behind in my rent. Finally, the manager came to me, telling me to pay up or leave. I had no choice—I had to go.

So I packed my few belongings in my battered suitcase and

decided to start walking after I got off work that night. I didn't know where I'd go, but I hoped that God would show me the way. I prayed for about half an hour that day, asking God to give me courage, keep me safe, and help me find work and a place to live. Then I went to the market—for what I thought would be the last time.

And it was. That evening, I met a woman who needed a live-in nanny, someone to take care of her three children. We talked for a while, and she gave me her address. I went by after work to meet her husband and children. We got along so well, she offered me the position. Now I not only had a well-paying job, I also had a place to live! I left the motel that night, not to walk a lonely road to places and things unknown, but to live with a family I came to love as my own. I was with them for two years, until I got married. We still keep in touch through letters and phone calls.

Who knows what they saved me from? I'd been at the end of my rope, and there's no telling what could have happened. I will always thank God for hearing my prayers—and answering them—that night.

—C.L., Texas

When my husband rushed home from work that spring day to tell me about his promotion to assistant manager, I had mixed feelings. Of course I was happy for him. But the past months had been sad for me. My mother had died a few months earlier, and, now, my husband's promotion meant a move away from our small town to a large city—away from our friends and the routine of a small town where I was born, went to school, fell in love, and got married. Other than not managing to start our family, that was how my life had been. My doctor had done some tests, and had found nothing wrong.

I'd been with my mother when she died, and I often thought about her last words: "Now you'll be looking after all the children." I had held her hand and whispered that I, too, was sure we'd soon have a family, but she had repeated, "No, no, dear. You'll be looking after *all* the children, *all* the dear precious souls." I knew I'd never forget her words or the sweetness and peace in her voice—and then she was gone.

I did my best to be happy in our new home, but I felt so alone. My husband was thrilled with his job and was meeting lots of new people. So I was very happy when he came in after work one Saturday saying, "I heard on the car radio that the hospital is looking for volunteers. You look over the list of help they need and choose what you'd like to do. What do you think?" Right away I liked the idea.

I was the first volunteer to show up that Monday morning. The counselor said they needed the most help at a residence type of hospital "for patients needing a lot of personal, one-on-one care." I went right over to meet the coordinator of volunteer work, and immediately felt I had found a friend. We chatted as we walked toward the activity building, and as we reached the glass doors, several patients rushed up, obviously happy to see the coordinator. Suddenly, I was surprised to realize that all of these patients were to some degree mentally retarded. When I turned to the coordinator, my face betrayed my surprise. She nodded her head and said, "Yes, they are all children, all such dear precious souls, and they so need our special loving care." I was looking straight into the woman's eyes, but her words echoed those of my mother.

That was all five years ago. We've made a good home here, and our nursery has had two occupants, a four-year-old son and a two-year-old daughter. Recently, I've resumed my visits to the hospital. My husband and I know we are blessed, and I know it even more every time I arrive at the hospital and see those faces light up when they recognize me.

And I always think about my mother's words, and, somehow, I know she is always there with me, and that God sent me a special message about caring and helping others through her.

—H.C., British Columbia, Canada

Everything had gone badly that day. I had a job interview at 9:30 A.M., but my little boy woke up feeling sick and I realized that chicken pox had finally made its way to our house. I phoned the personnel manager and asked to postpone my interview, but she told me that all interviews had to be held that day. The tears rolled down my cheeks as I hung up the phone. As a single mother I needed that job desperately.

By dinnertime it was clear that my other son had also caught the bug and I knew I would be busy the next few days playing nurse. Rather than worry about a paying job, I decided to devote myself completely to keeping my children comfortable. I alternated between reading stories and giving soothing baths to my two patients and cuddling them.

Each night after the boys went to sleep I prayed that God would find another job for me when I could finally go out looking again. I felt so trapped, so frustrated, and the ten days seemed endless.

Finally, when the boys were well again and went back to school, I set out to look for a job, confident that God would answer my prayers. I had always gone to church and sent the boys to Sunday school and felt that God owed it to me. Each evening I scanned the help-wanted ads, circling any positions that I sounded qualified for. I would take anything that could tide me over until a better job came along. Each morning I made phone calls, wrote letters of application, or attended interviews. Nothing. Nothing even close to a job.

About two weeks after the boys had returned to school, I got off the bus and walked the three blocks home. *Doesn't anyone want me?* I asked myself. *Am I really useless?*

As if I had spoken aloud, I heard a voice call to me, "Can you give me a hand?" It was our new neighbor, a member of the family who'd moved in a month before. We considered them very mysterious. There was seldom any movement outside the house, and with an automatic garage door, we didn't even get a good look at the occupants of the car when they went out.

But there was the voice, coming from the garage. As I approached, a little apprehensively, I saw a woman about my age trying to lift someone out of the car.

"Angela is having one of her bad days and doesn't want to get out of the car," the woman explained. "Maybe if you say something to her she'll cooperate."

Say something? What would I say? I didn't even know the child. "You look tired. Let's go inside and look at a book together."

Was that my voice speaking so soothingly? I wasn't conscious of saying anything, but that was my voice I heard. To my amazement the girl came willingly. She grabbed my hand and pulled me into the house. Her mother followed, whispering, "I can't believe it. She's never taken to anyone like that before."

The girl led me to a threadbare sofa, pointed, and said, "Dah." I sat down. She took a book from the coffee table and handed it to me. She snuggled contentedly beside me and looked at the pictures while I read. It wasn't long before I felt her head heavy on my shoulder and I realized I'd lost my audience.

Over coffee at the kitchen table, her mother told me about her twelve-year-old daughter. "She was brain damaged at birth and will never function beyond the level of a one-year-old. It is so hard to take her out anymore; she gets tired or stubborn and I just can't lift her. She looks like a normal child so people often look at me in disgust as if I can't control my child."

Before I realized what I'd said, I'd offered to stay with the girl while her mother shopped, did errands, or just needed time alone. I have never seen such a look of relief on anyone's face.

Later that night I shared my story with God. As I told Him about my new friend, I realized there must be many more women like my neighbor out there, trapped in their own homes for want of someone to help care for a loved one who couldn't stay alone.

It was only when I was almost asleep that I realized I'd forgotten to pray for a job. *Oh, well,* I thought, *God already knows I need income.* That night I slept more peacefully than I had in months.

As soon as I'd sent the boys off to school the next morning, I visited the local library and got out books on working with the disabled. Then I stopped at the newspaper office and placed an ad. It began: "Wanted: A Chance To Help You."

Now, one year later, I have my own business with three women working for me. Every day I thank God for answering my prayers.

—A.A., British Columbia, Canada

When I was a senior in high school, I found out I was pregnant. When the baby's father found out, he left town. He was twenty-three and I was seventeen. Foolishly, I had believed him when he said he loved me and that we would be married if I was to get pregnant.

I was able to finish high school with the help of a wonderful counselor, but I was terrified for my future and that of my baby. Well-meaning friends and family advised me to give up my baby for adoption. When I refused to consider it I was called a fool and told that my life was over, that no one would ever want me.

Night after night, I cried myself to sleep in shame, frustration, and fear. After one particularly ugly scene with my parents, I ran to my room and wept bitterly, all the while pleading into the dark, "Please help me. I don't know what to do anymore." Over and over I repeated the cry until I fell asleep from exhaustion.

The next morning when I awoke I felt peaceful for the first time in months. I emerged from my room refreshed, smiling, and totally at peace with myself. I knew, without a doubt, that my life was in the hands of God and that I might have hard work ahead of me, but I had nothing to fear.

A few months later I gave birth to a baby girl. She was big and beautiful and an absolute joy to everyone she came in contact with. Even Grandpa melted the first time she smiled at him. Then, before she was eight weeks old, a dear friend returned home from Vietnam. I had known John for over five years and had always loved him as my dearest friend, but it wasn't until his return from the war that I saw him as the wonderful man he had become.

All of this happened eighteen years ago. John and I will celebrate our seventeenth anniversary in April and our daughter graduates from high school in June. I have returned to school and will also graduate in June from junior college on my way to earning a BA degree.

This graduation, as I walk across the stage to receive my diploma, I'll remember another graduation eighteen years ago. Then the only ceremony I participated in was my counselor handing me a diploma as I held my baby in my arms and my faith in God in my heart. Now, as my family watches, I will close my eyes for a moment and say a silent, "Thank you," before I leave the stage in triumph.

—J.L.W., California

My grandmother was a pioneer woman. Born in 1853 in Kansas, she saw the Civil War from both sides as her brothers, with divided loyalties, fought against each other. As a young bride she traveled by wagon train to California and worked beside my grandfather to stake their claim. Two years later they crossed the country again and bought a farm in Pennsylvania. She was twenty-two years old when her husband died, leaving her with four young children to raise on her own.

Hardworking, thrifty, and fiercely independent, Gram worked the farm and raised her brood. She persevered through crop failures, two cases of diphtheria, and winters so cold she brought the chickens into the house to keep them from freezing. Each of her children attended a one-room school for the three R's, but she, herself, instilled in them the strong moral principles by which she had always lived.

An ideal grandmother, she kept us enthralled with stories of her early life. The Civil War, Indian attacks on the wagon train, the grandeur of the Rockies, and the blistering summer winds blowing across Kansas all came alive for us through her tales. Every recounting was followed by a Bible verse, which always referred in some way to courage, strength, or love.

"Remember," Gram had cautioned, "we are here to serve God, not to ask for special favors. He knows what is in your heart and will give it to you if He can."

I was married with two babies of my own when my grandmother turned ninety-five years old. She still lived alone, relying on others only for her groceries. However, we had discovered this incredibly brave lady did have one fear—that she might die alone. Since she refused to have telephone service, we shared that worry, but there was no way that we could change her mind. Gram wanted to live her own life—her own way, and because we loved her, we had to respect that. But we also were afraid that we might not be there with her when she needed us the most.

At six o'clock one November morning, one of Gram's neighbors called and told my mother to come at once. When we arrived at my grandmother's, three neighbors were there with her. Gram had awakened feeling ill, and had dressed and combed her hair, then turned on the table lamp by the window and pulled her chair beside it. For over an hour my grandmother had moved the window shade back and forth in a swaying motion hoping to attract attention. The early-rising neighbor just happened to spot the light and, realizing there was trouble, had called us.

Gram looked at us all gathered there with her and smiled faintly. She was holding my mother's hand when God called her. Truly, He had seen what was in her heart and had granted her that last wish.

—F. G., Florida

I had always had a strong faith in God, but it really began to waver when we went through a crisis that seemed to have no end. My husband had lost his job of thirty years, and he hadn't been able to find another. Our life's savings was quickly dwindling as we struggled to pay rent, utilities, groceries, and numerous other bills. We had six children, two of whom were still in school. Our life had never been easy, and we had always had a lot of bills. I had worked outside our home since our youngest child was one and a half, and after my husband lost his job I began working all the hours I could get as a waitress in a large hotel. I made good money, but we still had to take money from our savings every month just to make ends meet.

One night, after my husband had been unemployed for seven months, I reached my lowest and felt my faith slipping far away. I was driving home from work—I was tired, depressed, and thinking about all our bills that had been piling up. Our rent was due the next day and the only way I could pay it was to draw from our savings again. We had nine hundred dollars left, and I had wanted to keep that for emergencies.

Suddenly it all got the best of me and I began to cry and beg God to show me the way. I told Him I didn't care if we had a dime saved if only we could just somehow hang on and take care of things. I begged Him to help me talk to our landlord and work something out, and I asked Him to help my husband find something, anything to do—his unemployment was running out and then what would we do? I said, "Lord, I can't cope anymore. Please show me the way. Give me some kind of sign." I was really upset, and it's a wonder I didn't have a wreck.

But then, suddenly, I was calm and I heard a voice. I even turned to look in the seat next to me because the voice was very distinct. He said only two words: "Fear not." I knew it was the voice of God speaking to me, and I cannot describe the incredible feeling that came over me. It was something that only those who have experienced it could know.

I went home, contacted my landlord, explained our situation, told him when I could pay the rent, and promised to do so at that time. I kept that promise. My husband was contacted the very next day by several different companies he'd interviewed with, and he went to work before a month was up. Though that job was seasonal and lasted only six months, it was only three weeks after it had ended that a longtime friend called my husband about a job in another state that was in the same line of work he had done for thirty years. We jumped at the chance, moved, and are still living very happily here today.

Now, whenever I'm feeling low, all I need to do is remember that night over two years ago when God spoke to me. I know that He was always with me, it was me who fell by the wayside.

—S.G., Arkansas

I have been a school nurse in a small southern town for twenty years. I have turned to God many times, but several years ago I really found out what true faith in God can accomplish.

One day a little eight-year-old child came into the school clinic and asked me to look at her leg. I expected a cut or a burn, so when I pulled down her pants, I almost fainted. From her knee to her groin was the most hideous growth I'd ever seen. My first thought was that it was cancer. I took her to the local pediatrician and she sent us to a surgeon. He took one look and said he felt sure the leg would have to be amputated. He thought it was cancer too.

I knew the child's background. Her mother was dead and her

father had deserted all of the children and moved north. The kids all lived in a shack in an alley, existing on what an elderly grandmother could spare and what they could salvage from garbage cans.

The doctor had said that because the child had one living parent, we had to find him to sign the consent papers for surgery. It looked hopeless. I took the child back to school and watched as she limped into the building. I put my head down on the steering wheel of my car and prayed this prayer: "Lord, I am helpless in this situation. I need Your guiding hand to help me help this child. Use me, Lord, in whatever way it takes to perform a miracle." As I lifted my head and turned on the car radio, I heard a man's voice say, "Bear ye one another's burden and so fulfill the law of Christ."

The next day I went to our school's district office, and we called the highway patrol in several northern states. They located the child's father, and within forty-eight hours he was on a bus, on his way to sign the consent papers. For a week it was almost like living in a dream world. Every door opened to me. The doctor operated for free, the hospital did not charge a dime, and most miraculous of all—the growth was benign and the leg was saved!

This happened during the Christmas season that year, and I believe it showed the real meaning of Christmas—helping others and changing lives. I know my life changed that week because I saw what the power of prayer and the miracle of faith can do!

—F.H.M., South Carolina

❖

Before I was wheeled out of the recovery room, my surgeon leaned over and said to me, "As far as I'm concerned, you are cured. But don't thank me," he added. "God healed you. I was only His instrument." The thrilling words penetrated my consciousness and I gripped his outstretched hand as I returned his broad smile.

Two weeks before, in my family physician's office, I was told I had a tumor the size of a golf ball on one ovary. The doctor told me that it would have to be removed as soon as possible.

The implications of this were devastating to me. In a daze, I took an ultrasound test and the results were not reassuring. My physician said the tumor was two inches in diameter and firmly attached to my right ovary. I asked the doctor if this might indicate a malignancy.

"Yes, it does," he answered. Then he added, "Frankly, I'm worried."

I chose a gynecologist to perform the surgery, which was scheduled for the following week. During the days prior to my surgery, I had numerous preoperative tests such as X-rays, blood tests, and a cardiogram. I also called the elders of our church, and they anointed me with oil and prayed for my complete healing, by whatever means God chose to use.

By the time I was taken into the operating room, I felt peaceful and unafraid. My next awareness was when the surgeon leaned over me in the recovery room and told me I was cured.

Hours later, in my hospital room, the surgeon told me that when he opened me up on the operating table, he found only a very small shriveled-up tumor hanging by a threadlike substance to a perfectly healthy ovary. He smiled as he told me that all he'd had to do was snip it off.

Two days later the lab report showed the tumor was not malignant and there was no sign of cancer. Faith does make a difference, and God *is* still performing miracles today. I know that He caused that tumor to shrivel up. My outlook on life has changed, and my priorities have been changed. Because of what happened to me, I have a new appreciation for family and friends, and for all the people that I meet.

—H. R., Michigan

I was not prepared for the news of my daughter's miscarriage when my son-in-law Bill called. Linda was my youngest daughter, and I had just seen her the day before. She was healthy and happy, and everything seemed to be fine.

On the way to the hospital, I prayed for my daughter. Although I knew she would be heartbroken, I wasn't too worried about her physical health. Miscarriages are rarely complicated, or so I thought at the time.

But I soon found out that Bill didn't tell me everything over the phone. Because of a tragic mistake, Linda hadn't received an adequate supply of oxygen to her brain, and she was now in a coma.

My heart ached as I looked at my daughter. She was once a lively girl who was a cheerleader in high school. She could never sit still when there was so much living to do.

Anger and denial flooded my mind. As I cried out in anguish to God, I felt the comfort of His presence, and I heard the promise, "She is going to be all right." In the days, weeks, and months that followed, these words sustained me.

As our friends and relatives learned about Linda's condition, they joined us in praying for her recovery. It was comforting to know we were not alone and that others cared and understood our pain.

My daughter was later moved out of the intensive-care unit and into a private room. We arranged our schedules so that one of us could always be with her. The doctors continued tests on her brain to determine any change or improvement.

After a month, the doctors told us that Linda would either remain in a coma or, if she regained consciousness, she would be a vegetable. They advised us to place her in a nursing home. But I remembered God's promise, and my mind was at peace.

We would always talk to Linda and believe that she could hear us, even though the medical staff told us not to expect any response. I was longing to know if she was aware of my presence.

When I told the nurse this, she suggested, "Tell her to blink her eyelids if she can hear you."

I did, and we anxiously waited for her response. After a minute, she opened and closed her eyes. I was filled with joy.

I leaned over and told her, "Linda, you are going to be all right."

From that point on, there was no looking back or giving up. With prayer, therapy, and love, my daughter began to improve and respond. Her recovery was slow, but she did recover. She painfully learned how to walk and talk again, feed and dress herself, and all the basic things that she had forgotten.

WHEREVER YOU GO, THERE HE IS

When I think of her then and look at her now, eight years later, I know that my faith and hope in God helped her recover. She is a lovely young woman with a full life ahead of her.

—D.G., North Carolina

It seemed like my world was falling apart when my doctor told me that my two-year-old daughter had leukemia. I could not believe what he was telling me. I knew that she'd had her cold and cough for a long time, but I thought it was just a bad case of the flu. It never even crossed my mind that she could have leukemia.

As I sat in his office, the doctor was explaining the blood-test results he had just received. Then he told me that he wanted to do a bone-marrow test on my baby. When he started telling me about the procedure, I couldn't listen anymore. I already knew how painful it was because my father had gone through the test a few years ago.

With tears running down my face, I thought to myself: *Oh, God, this can't be happening!* I told the doctor that I wanted the blood tests repeated before I would consent to the bone-marrow test. Reluctantly, he agreed.

Still in a state of shock, I took my little girl home. I walked around the house with her in my arms, praying constantly. I couldn't put her down. I was afraid if I did, I would surely lose her.

At night, my husband and I and our two older children would all hold hands with our baby girl and pray for her. The more we all prayed, the better I felt. I knew that God answered prayers, but what we were asking for was truly a miracle.

Three days after the second blood test was taken, the doctor called and told me to come in immediately. He refused to give me any information over the phone.

Before we left for his office, I held my baby tight and prayed like I had never prayed before. I poured my heart out to God and prayed all the way to the doctor's office.

We finally arrived, and as I sat there with my daughter in my arms, a very warm feeling spread through my body. I knew that whatever happened, God was there with me and my baby.

The doctor walked in, sat down, and finally spoke to me. "Mary, I don't understand this," he said. "Your baby's test was one hundred percent positive the first time, but the second test we've done is one hundred percent negative. I've had three other doctors review the test results with me, and everything is negative. I even had the blood tested twice."

With a smile on my face and joy in my heart, I told him, "Doctor, I think I understand. Maybe the tests you first ran were not right. Something must have gone wrong, and I am glad I had you take them over."

The doctor smiled and shook his head since he was as happy as I was.

Because of the constant faith that my family and I had in God, we knew He heard our prayers. We all have continued our belief in Him, and with His help, my little girl is now a beautiful and healthy eighteen-year-old woman.

—M.E.S., Pennsylvania

The nightmare came out of nowhere, a horror springing up in the midst of the happiest, loveliest year of my life. I had been married for two years to the only man I'd ever loved, and I had a healthy baby daughter who was about to celebrate her first birthday. I felt doubly, triply blessed, as though God Himself held me protectively in the hollow of His hand, assuring my contentment and clearing my path of all sorrow and distress.

And then with a suddenness that jarred my very soul, it was as if He had turned that hand over and let me fall.

We had just returned home late one evening from a week-long stay at my mother's farm. My husband, Brian, unlocked the front door and then took the sleeping baby from me as I reached into the mailbox to get the week's accumulated mail. I walked into the darkened living room ahead of Brian and switched on the lights. The mail dropped from my hand and scattered to the floor as I gasped in disbelief.

The living room was a shambles: furniture overturned, books flung everywhere, the drawers of the desk pulled out, their contents ransacked and thrown in every direction. I was about to say something to Brian when a sudden movement off to the left caught my eye. Then everything was a blur of motion. I briefly saw a face, a boy's face, tough and terrified, peering out from behind the couch. Then the boy rose and pivoted toward me. I caught a glimpse of something black in his hand, then there was a flash and a deafening roar. A searing pain pierced my abdomen. I lurched back with the impact of the bullet and sagged to the carpet. I remember thinking, as I sank into unconsciousness, how glad I was that I hadn't been holding the baby.

The next few days were a confusing torment. I would thrash in fitful, feverish sleep, then rise to a groggy half-consciousness. In that state, I could make out the hospital room around me and the doctors and nurses who seemed to be hovering continually and anxiously nearby. Mostly, though, I was in a state between unconsciousness and full alertness, a place plagued by dreams and strange thoughts, where I couldn't always tell the difference between imagination and reality, fact and fancy. At one point, I thought that I heard Brian's voice, distraught and weary, and a doctor explaining to him about a fragmented bullet, about massive internal damage, about the need for yet another operation. I heard someone else whisper that it was touch and go.

I remember struggling to wake up, but finding that the sedatives I'd been given were too strong. Fear clutched at my mind. Yet something even more powerful had taken control of my heart: Hatred.

Floating before my burning brain was that insolent, youthful face, the sneering, hardened look that the intruder, that boy, had given me as he reared to shoot me. How I hated him! How dare he enter my life unasked, only to ruin it. How dare he destroy our property, endanger my family, leave my baby without a mother, my husband without a wife. An unquenchable desire for revenge seized hold of me. I wanted that punk to suffer as he had made me suffer. Anger and hatred merged with my physical wound to become a permanent, aching fire in the center of my soul.

And then something marvelous happened. On the evening of what I later learned was my fourth day in the hospital, my usually restless, shallow sleep became deep and calm, and the chaotic jumble in my mind gave way to a vivid dream of stunning clarity. I was standing before a light. It was extremely bright, yet it did not hurt my eyes at all to look directly at it. And out of that light came a voice, very firm and authoritative, but gentle also, the way a strong father might sound when talking to his child. It was a voice speaking in a tone of command, though not at all threatening, and it said very distinctly, "Forgive the boy."

I was aghast. In my dream, I shouted back, "Forgive him? Forgive the person who shot me, who might have killed my husband, my child? I can't. I'll never feel anything but hatred for him."

"Forgive the boy," the voice repeated.

"No!" I screamed.

"Forgive the boy," the voice intoned. "Forgive those who trespass against you, that you might be forgiven your trespasses. It is the way."

Still I resisted. Every fiber of my being recoiled at the thought of forgiving one who had done me such a terrible wrong. But the voice, ever firm and clear, persisted, until at last I began to understand. My hatred was depleting my energy, twisting my mind, using up bodily and spiritual resources necessary for my healing. Until I released my anger, relinquished my thirst for vengeance, I could not be saved. God would not heal someone so full of hatred as I.

The realization brought with it a soothing peacefulness, a restfulness I had not experienced since the shooting. The light, the dream—it all vanished as I climbed swiftly to complete wakefulness. "I forgive him," I said distinctly, as my eyes opened and I looked into the startled face of a young nurse bending over me.

The calm joy I felt when I made that admission swept over my fevered body like cool water. The terrible pain in my abdomen broke and faded. After that, recovery was quick and sure. I was out of the hospital two weeks later.

The first thing I did when I recovered was to prove to myself and everyone else that I truly was forgiving. Eddie, the boy who shot me, had been apprehended by the police just days before I was released, and, though Brian was opposed at first, I involved myself in his case. I learned that Eddie was a troubled youngster, the child of an alcoholic mother and a father who had abandoned the family when Eddie was three. Now seventeen, Eddie wasn't really bad, just confused and lonely, a wayward boy who'd fallen in with the wrong crowd. It turned out that our house was the very first one he had ever broken into, and his firing the gun had been the result of panic, not viciousness.

Thanks to my intercession, the judge agreed to reduce the charges against Eddie and put him on a probationary rehabilitation program in which he does community-service work in lieu of jail time. Brian and I have both befriended him. Suspicious at first, Eddie couldn't understand what was making us act in a way he'd never seen humans act before in his entire life. I tried to explain to him about my dream, about my belief that God had spoken directly to me, urging me to truly practice the faith I had been claiming to possess all these years. God had reminded me that love and forgiveness have to be the core of that faith, or it means nothing at all.

I think that Eddie is beginning to understand. Last month he was baptized a member of our church, and our minister revealed to me afterward that this former "bad boy" had asked about the possibility of entering a seminary after high school!

—K.F., Ohio

It had snowed, and it was so cold in the bedroom of our log cabin, my fingers were numb as I hurriedly dressed. I could hear my husband trying to get that stubborn old stove to give more heat. No matter how hard we tried, it was just too old to adequately heat our small cabin.

I looked over at our five-year-old daughter, sleeping. We had brought her home from the hospital the previous day. She had survived another bout of pneumonia, one of many she'd suffered that miserable winter. She opened her eyes and smiled. I quickly dressed her in warm clothes, and we hurried to huddle around the feeble heat.

We ate breakfast sitting around the stove. We had given up trying to eat our meals at the table. Money was so short this year, since our daughter's hospital stays had taken every cent we could make above necessities. My husband repeated the words he had said to me so often. "I sure wish we could buy that heater our neighbor has for sale. It would really keep this house warm."

Our daughter asked, "Daddy, do you want a new stove?"

My husband looked down at her and smiled. "Well, it would sure be a godsend, but I'm afraid we can't afford it right now." She told him not to worry, that she'd just ask God for the stove.

She knelt beside her bed. Her hands were folded beneath her chin, and her lips were moving. In a short while, she came out, kissed each of us, and said, "We will have a new stove soon."

That day, a lady we had met at church was at our door. She brought blankets, and warm clothes for our daughter. I opened the stove to put more wood on the struggling fire. Our guest said,

"That stove doesn't throw much heat, does it?" I told her that we would like to get another as soon as we could. She asked me if the one our neighbor was selling was the right kind. When I told her that was the stove we were planning on getting, she wanted to go take a look.

Our neighbor showed us the stove. To me it was beautiful. The woman from church asked me if I liked it and I told her it was the nicest stove I had ever seen. She immediately paid for it, over my protests. She said that God told us to help each other.

After work, my husband brought the stove home. In no time the new stove was burning brightly. At dinner, we were able to sit at the table and enjoy our meal. We thanked the Lord and our friend from church for the stove.

Our daughter said, "I'll be right back. I've got to thank the Lord myself." As she knelt beside her bed again, the thought raced through my mind, "And a child shall lead them." It only proves once more that God does indeed work in mysterious ways.

—E.L.R., California

My mother's arthritis progressed to a debilitating state by the time she reached eighty-two. She'd had several falls, and I finally convinced her to move in with my husband and me.

After taking her to a number of specialists and for numerous tests, she was diagnosed as having osteoarthritis. The doctor recommended medication and physical therapy four times a week for the next four to six weeks.

I was already a busy housewife engaged in two part-time jobs and many other activities. Now I was burdened with the additional responsibility of caring for my invalid mother. Naturally, I was bitter and resentful. I was weary of being burdened with heavy crosses all my life.

Then I felt ashamed of my bitterness. It was my mother, after all, who'd encouraged me throughout my life to be a responsible, God-loving person. I prayed to God to remove the anger, hurt, and bitterness. He heard my prayers, and slowly, a miracle occurred within me.

As each day moved into the next, I began to look forward to the trips to therapy with Mom. Each person was genuinely motivated to work hard in physical therapy to improve their health. During the hours I waited for my mother to complete her therapy, I caught up on my reading, and I prayed and contemplated God and my blessings. This became my private time with God.

I truly realized that the crosses I'd been given to bear were challenges to make me more aware. I changed from a growling, complaining person, to one open to the experience. By attempting to handle this burden, I actually became grateful instead of bitter.

And so I prayed: "Thank you God for this opportunity to help my mother, and to see her health improve. Thank you for enabling me to know and love you better and serve you happily. Thank you for permitting this change to happen inside me."

The greatest reward occurred the day my mother no longer needed her walker and relied only on her cane. The doctor discharged her from the hospital and she was permitted to return home.

Mom looked at me with misty eyes and spoke. "Thank you for helping me get better. I love you, dear daughter."

Tears tightened in my throat, but I managed to say, "Thank you, Lord, for making us *both* better."

—D.A., Pennsylvania

When I was in college, I thought we'd live forever and nothing bad could ever happen to us. It was winter and my roommate and I were having fun, drinking and driving down the mountain. The road was a series of sharp S-turns, each one sharper than the last as we descended the mountain.

All of a sudden, my friend cried out that she didn't have any brakes! We sped through the first curve, the car taking on a life of its own. The brakes wouldn't hold. We were going faster and faster. We both feared we wouldn't make that last curve. At the bottom of the mountain was a sheer forty-foot drop.

I had been raised in a religious home, but I wasn't leading a religious life. The moment I was looking death in the face was the only time in a year that I had thought of God. At twenty years old, religion had no place in my life.

In an instant, I saw my sister on her knees, praying to God to keep me safe. I could see her as clearly as if she were there in the car with me, racing down the mountain at breakneck speed. I could see the tears in her eyes as she cried, "Lord, please save her!"

I told my friend to keep hitting the brakes. We were coming to the last curve, both of us crying and screaming. All of a sudden, the car started to slow down. The brakes were holding! The car slowed until it came to a complete stop about ten feet from the stop sign at the bottom of the mountain. We sat there for a while staring up at the night sky and thanking God that we were alive. Neither one of us spoke a word as we drove home.

A week later, it hit home hard when I received a letter from my sister, who lived in another country. In the first line, she asked if I was alright. She said that last Saturday night she had awoken from a sound sleep. She had a dream that I was crashing down the side of a mountain. My sister got up from bed and knelt down to pray for me, asking the Lord to keep me safe.

I showed that letter to my friend who was driving the car. We both cried together.

Now as I look back on my early years, I realize that the scene of my sister praying for me was relived many times in my life. As my own children grow, I rely on prayer to keep them safe. When I wake up in the middle of the night, I don't just turn over and go back to sleep—I pray to God for His will to be done. I pray for my loved ones to be safe from all harm, in His arms. So they will have time to get their lives on track, like I did. Prayer for our loved ones is the most powerful gift we can give our family.

—C.P., Mississippi

MEMBERS' STORIES

One beautiful morning, while my ten-year-old twin daughters and their six-year-old sister were at school, I was hurrying to get my housework underway and feed my little two-year-old boy. There was always more to do than I thought was possible in a day's time. Once the wash was in the washer and the little one fed and put down for his nap, the dishes were next on my list of things to do.

The baby, Lee, didn't care what room in the house I was in as long as he could hear me sing, so I sang as I worked, in case he was still awake. I filled the sink with hot, soapy water and began to wash the dishes and sing to Lee at first, then the singing turned into praises to God. I sang as if I were an opera star, and I felt so full of God's Holy Spirit, I thought I was going to burst. I was so filled with the love of the Lord that all I wanted to do was sing His praises.

While I was singing, I felt a presence in my kitchen. I stopped and turned around, only to see my refrigerator. Nothing and no one was in the room, so I began to sing praises again, only to feel a presence all too real. A voice not audible but very clear, as if from their mind into mine, said, "Would you raise a son for me?"

At this point, I was thinking I must be crazy. I replied, "I can't have a son; I had a hysterectomy when I was twenty-eight." Again the voice asked, "Would you raise a son for me?" I replied, "I already have a son." Again, "Would you raise a son for me?" My reply this time was, "Lord, if this is you, then I will raise a son for you. I will do whatever you want me to do."

As quickly as I had felt His presence and heard His words, this precious time had passed. I started to cry. I needed to talk to someone, but felt like whomever I called would think I was crazy. There was one person I could talk to, because she was a Christian and loved the Lord just as I did—my friend Naomi. I called Naomi and asked her just to listen as I told her what happened to me. After I had finished, her answer to me was, "If I were you, I would be expecting a little boy. The Bible is not just for yesterday, it is for yesterday, today, and tomorrow, until Jesus comes back. He can and does talk to us if we will listen, and you must have been listening. Anything that has happened in biblical times can and does happen today." I expected to get a little boy to raise right away, but that didn't happen for many years.

My twins, Sharon and Karron, grew up and married. Sharon became separated from her husband while she was pregnant, and came back home to live. She had a beautiful little boy with jet black hair and big brown eyes who she named Michael. My husband and I fell in love with him. Sharon and Michael lived with us until Michael was three years old, when they moved to Texas to live with our youngest daughter, Anita. About eleven months later, Lee Senior and I were going on vacation and went to see our children in Texas. When our visit was over, Lee and I were in our car talking to Sharon and ready to leave when Michael said he wanted to get into the car also. Sharon let him sit in the backseat while we were talking, but when we were ready to leave, Michael didn't want to get out of the car. He told his mother he was going home with BeBop and Granddad. Sharon agreed to let him go just for a little while, which was all we thought it would be.

Michael came home with us. Sharon called each week to see if he was ready to come home to Texas, but he would not go. At church one Sunday, Naomi came out of her class when she saw Michael and me, and wanted to know if I thought this was the son that God was going to send me. "No," I answered, "this is my grandson, Michael." Lee and I had already raised four children and were not too excited about starting all over again. Little did I know Michael would never go home to Texas.

Sharon would not have very long to live. She died at thirty-six years old. We adopted Michael and what joy he has given us! He was one of the leaders in the F.C.A. Christian organization at school, played football, was in ROTC, and went to Paraguay to do mission work in his sophomore year. Although we have lost Sharon, we know where she is. I have often thought I would have loved for Sharon to have known and shared the love Michael has shared with us, but that was not God's plan. He wanted Sharon in heaven and Michael in our home: He already told me so.

Yes, Lord, I did raise a son for you. Thank you for that son.

—E.P., Kentucky

I have been a single parent now for fifteen years. New Year's Eve 1998 I was feeling really lonely. My two youngest daughters were staying with some friends for the night. My youngest son was staying with his father in Montana over the holiday, and my oldest two children lived on their own. Even the two handicapped ladies I take care of were asleep down the hall.

It was around 11:45 P.M. when it hit me. Another new year and we were doing okay, but I was working three jobs to make ends meet. I was so tired. I started to cry and then I started to pray: "Dear Lord, how am I going to make it through another year?" I felt so helpless. All of a sudden, I felt these comforting arms go around me. I couldn't see anyone, but I know it was my heavenly Father there to comfort me, and let me know everything was going to be alright.

We have had our ups and downs since then, but I won't give up, because I know that even though you can't see Him, He will always be there for you.

—S.E., Idaho

I have read your many testimonies with great interest. They reminded me of an occurrence years ago that left me with no doubt that I was protected by God's grace.

I was in the habit of traveling thirty miles every week with my two small sons to a Bible meeting in another town. This was in Kansas, and it was usual to go seventy miles per hour on the long, straight roads there. Every week I would put two dollars' worth of gas in the car to get us there and back and it always did—until one night after dark when I was five miles from home. Suddenly, I felt my foot hit the floorboard. I realized I had run out of gas.

I pulled over to the side of the road. As I did so, I became aware of a small dip in the road ahead, which I could not have seen if I had not accidentally run out of gas at that exact spot. I was able to make out a crossing with many cows on the road right where I would have been driving. Soon I heard a car behind me and the brakes screaming as the driver tried to stop. By this time, though, the animals were up on the straight of the road and were seen in time for the driver to stop. But when I ran out of gas, stopping the car was the only way I could have seen those cows in the dip of the road.

I drove that road safely many times before and after, and I feel sure I was protected by our Lord from harm.

—V.B., California

❖

My fifteen-year-old son, Jeremy, was diagnosed with leukemia in October 1996. The first night in the hospital was terrifying.

Late that night, after Jeremy was allowed to go to sleep, I was sitting by the window, looking out and crying. I had barely gotten the words "Lord, I'm scared" out of my mouth when I felt a presence in the room. I heard a voice say, "Don't worry. He's going to be okay."

It was a long, hard road, and we almost lost Jeremy twice: first, when he wanted to give up several months into his treatment, and then again when he got a bacterial infection. He was in ICU for five days in a drug-induced coma. The first day the doctors told us Jeremy was a very sick young man and that there was a good chance we would lose him.

I remembered the voice and somehow knew my son would survive. Praise Almighty God! Today, my son is a happy, healthy twenty-two-year-old who loves to tease his dad and me and argue with his eighteen-year-old sister.

Never doubt that our God can do what he says He can do. Just love and trust him. He'll see you through whatever trials come in our way. God never promised us a rose garden, just that He will hold our hands and help us through the thorns of life, if we only trust Him.

—S.M., Texas

hen Samuel took a stone and set it up between Mizpay and Shen. He named it Ebenezer, saying 'Thus far has the Lord helped us.' " (1 Samuel 7:12)

Following is my Ebenezer stone. Whenever I think of it, I remember my visit from God and know that he loves and cares for me.

Mom died about ten years ago. She had been in the last stages of Alzheimer's disease and her death was a welcome blessing— we all knew she would be going Home. My life, however, was a torment. I was in a terrible marriage and was extremely unhappy. As insensitive as it may sound, being around my large extended family for my mother's funeral gave me some much-needed time away from home. I was glad to be among people who loved me.

It was cold in Pittsburgh in November. There was a layer of snow that just covered the streets and made the sidewalks slippery. Nevertheless, I needed to be by myself for awhile and try to sort things out. The woods in front of my sister's house provided the perfect place for a quiet secluded walk. I was in deep despair. To this day, I can still remember the anguish I felt as I walked along, trying to connect with God. Maybe, I thought, if I sat down and concentrated—that was it—walking along the slippery path took a lot of concentration as it was.

I found a log, brushed off the snow, and sat down. I had promised my sister that I would be back in forty-five minutes, without fail. I looked at my watch to check the time and then started to pour out my soul to God. I begged Him to send me a sign that He was listening. Just at that time, a red cardinal (incidentally, my favorite bird because they are so pretty and bright), landed on a branch not two feet away from me. I did not think too much about that except I expected the bird to fly away in a few seconds since it had landed so close to a human being.

I continued to talk to God, imploring Him to help me. I kept my eye on the bird since it was so close but it remained on the branch. At times I prayed out loud, and at others I spoke from my heart. All the while, the cardinal stayed close to me. After a while, I checked my watch. I had been sitting there for twenty minutes and so had the cardinal. It never moved from the branch. I got up to leave, and the cardinal flew to a higher branch. Never would I have believed that a wild bird would stay near a human being—in one place—for twenty minutes. As I finished my walk I knew that God Himself had visited me.

Did life get miraculously better? No. But it did get better. In the ensuing years, I have used this event as my Ebenezer stone. Whenever I am troubled or think that God has forgotten me, I remember His loving visit to me ten years ago and know He will never leave nor forsake me, as He has promised.

—C.W., Florida

The Lord Jesus heard my cries and delivered me from the horrors of alcoholic addiction. This is my accurate version of the circumstances.

"Get away! Stay away from me!" I shouted at the grotesque monsters endlessly approaching my bed. "What do you want from me? Please go away!"

Racing into the hallway, I doubled over in pain, vomiting on the beautiful new carpet. I crawled back into bed, scratching myself raw from the continuous bugs slithering over my skin. I had only planned to have a drink or two. Why did alcohol hit me so fast?

Shivering in bed, freezing one minute and burning the next, I looked back at the jobs and friends lost, and relationships ended before they began. What was wrong with me? I was given a fine education, but no one ever told me about a disease called "alcoholism." Hospitals and self-help groups help many. Unfortunately, not me. Now I was in the hospital again, this time with cirrhosis of the liver.

My friend asked, "Have you ever tried God?"

"I believe in God, but I don't think he's too fond of me at the moment," I answered.

He told me if I believed that I should know:

". . . neither death nor life, neither angels nor demons, neither the present nor the future, nor any powers neither height nor depth, nor anything else in all creation, will ever be able to separate us from the love of God that is in Christ Jesus our Lord." (Romans 8:38)

One night, the horrifying monsters returned, coming ceaselessly from the wall, terrifying me, making my blood run cold with fear. Drenched in perspiration, I fell on my knees and cried out, "God, please help me. Make them go away. I can't go through this any longer."

I stayed crumpled on the floor for some time, then slowly climbed into bed, falling into a dreamless sleep. Though I was ill for several days after that, the sickness was never more than I could bear.

That was several years ago, and since then the desire to drink has never recurred. God heard my cries. All I was asking for was the power to resist temptation, but God went one better and took the temptation completely away. My doctor is amazed, as chronic alcoholism is never cured instantaneously. Truly, I received a miracle!

Today I live with the peace that passes all understanding, free of that horrible addiction, for *"If the Son sets you free, you will indeed be free."* (John 8:36)

—C.D., California

F eeling the presence of Jesus is becoming more profound for me every day and writing about it gives me unbelievable joy! If I were to tell about one particularly special time I felt the Lord's presence, it would have to be in the ICU waiting room sometime during the night of October 20, 2001.

Our only son, Timothy, had been in a one-vehicle accident and had suffered blunt-force trauma to his head, injuring the left side of his brain and causing his right frontal lobe to swell, thus putting enormous pressure on his brain. An earlier operation became a futile attempt to relieve that intense pressure and Tim continued to remain critical. The myriad desperate feelings we had to overcome were quite apparent—our twenty-six-year-old son, gifted in architecture and music, was going to die.

Tim had recently earned his Master of Architecture and was happily working to make a difference in his local community. He had been out on a short errand with his girlfriend when the accident occurred. That night in October forever changed my life and wounded my mother's heart. Through all the pain, however, I can still testify to God's unfailing love and goodness toward my family.

Late during the night of October 20th, surrounded by a prayer circle of friends, young and old, and our former pastor, our small family sat in the dimly lit waiting room. One other family was "camped out" at the other end of the very long room. We had just been told by the neurosurgeon that Tim's chances to survive were slim, and we were asked if we had considered organ donation. It was a harsh thought, but also a realistic possibility since he was so very healthy. From out of nowhere, a beautiful tall woman came to us and was led to pray for our situation. Her daughter was in the bed next to Tim's and she had serious circumstances to overcome too. I remember a close circle, powerful words lifted up in prayer, unbelievable supernatural strength, and undoubtedly THE POWER OF THE HOLY SPIRIT'S PRESENCE!

We overcame any doubt to donate Tim's organs and as a result, he saved seven people's lives through the gifts of his corneas, pancreas, liver, and kidneys. Tim's sister, my husband, and I all praise God and thank Him daily for His unfailing love in the form of a prayer warrior when we needed her the most.

—P.T., Texas

A Letter to Our Readers

Dear Reader:

In order that we might better contribute to your reading enjoyment, we would appreciate your taking a few minutes to respond to the following questions. When completed, please return to the following:

Andrea Doering, Editor-in-Chief
Crossings Book Club
401 Franklin Avenue, Garden City, NY 11530

You can post your review online! Go to www.crossings.com and rate this book.

Title _____ Author _____

1 Did you enjoy reading this book?

❑ Very much. I would like to see more books by this author!

❑ I really liked_____

❑ Moderately. I would have enjoyed it more if_____

2 What influenced your decision to purchase this book? Check all that apply.

    ❑ Cover
    ❑ Title
    ❑ Publicity
    ❑ Catalog description
    ❑ Friends
    ❑ Enjoyed other books by this author
    ❑ Other _____

3 Please check your age range:

    ❑ Under 18   ❑18-24
    ❑ 25-34   ❑ 35-45
    ❑ 46-55   ❑ Over 55

4 How many hours per week do you read? _____

5 How would you rate this book, on a scale from 1 (poor) to 5 (superior)?
_____

Name_____

Occupation_____

Address_____

City_____ State_____ Zip_____